D1071569

The 46th Star

The 46th Star

A History of Oklahoma's Constitutional Convention and Early Statehood

by

Irvin Hurst

Western Heritage Books, Inc.
Oklahoma City 1980

Affectionately Dedicated
to
Marion
And Our Children
Randle, Owen and Carol

Originally published by Semco Color Press, Inc., Oklahoma City.

Manufactured in the United States of America.

ISBN: 0-86546-011-6

A Foreword Postscript

Oklahoma has added 23 years since *The 46th Star* first appeared, and many of my friends then living, who participated in events leading to statehood, have since departed. But accounts of their various roles in establishing "not merely a new state" but "a new kind of state" have grown in interest. Once the first printing of *The 46th Star* was exhausted, the demand (and price, for the occasional copy found in a used book store) increased.

The invitations for after-dinner talks also have kept pace, and the author has found audiences, many woefully lacking in accurate knowledge of major events, eager to hear the true story. Few realized that it was just four days short of a year from the day the Constitutional Convention met in Guthrie — November 20, 1906 — until statehood came on November 16, 1907. And hundreds, fed on distorted stories about how the capital was "stolen" from Guthrie, learned for the first time that the capital removal campaign covered a period of 20 years. Recognition came from both the *Encyclopedia Brittanica* and the *Americana* which now credit *The 46th Star* with source material.

So it is with pride that the author offers this second printing for the enlightenment of a new generation many of whom will live to see Oklahoma celebrate its 100th birthday.

IRVIN HURST

Acknowledgements

In compiling the material in this volume, the author had generous assistance from many sources. Special thanks are due the following:

Three survivors of the Constitutional Convention, former Gov. Henry S. Johnston, Rev. Henry L. Cloud and Hon. William C. Liedtke; and to Mrs. John B. Harrison, whose husband served in the convention and later became chief justice of the State Supreme Court.

The staff of the Oklahoma Historical Society, and particularly to Mrs. Elsie D. Hand, librarian, who stayed late hours to permit the author to continue his research; Mrs. O. J. Cook, in charge of the newspaper file room; Mrs. C. E. Cook, curator of the museum, and to Dow Jenkins, the janitor, who ignored "quitting time" so the author could continue perusual of the early newspaper files.

The staff of the Secretary of State, and particularly to Jeff Kendall, assistant secretary, and Mrs. Dolly Dahlgren.

Miss Frances Haskell, daughter of the first governor.

Stanley Draper, Managing Director of Oklahoma City Chamber of Commerce.

Massena Murray and former Gov. Johnston Murray, sons of the convention president and later governor, William H. "Alfalfa Bill" Murray.

Miss Florence O. Wilson, niece of W. F. Harn.

Dr. T. Bruce Robb, Kansas City, Mo., author of "The Guaranty of Bank Deposits."

Charles L. Fuson, secretary of the Oklahoma Bankers Association.

Floyd Maytubby, Governor of the Chickasaws.

Russell R. Berry, assistant in the State Library.

Paul Bennett, vice president of Semco Color Press.

The Saturday Evening Post.

And while he is departed, to William H. "Alfalfa Bill" Murray for his personal anecdotes over the years and for the excellent material in "Memoirs of Governor Murray and the True History of Oklahoma."

—The Author.

Foreword

ALL OF OKLAHOMA'S FORMER GOVERNORS were still living when as a young reporter I was first assigned to cover the capitol. One day early in the William H. Murray administration—late 1931 or early 1932—a man with graying hair, somewhat heavy-set but distinguished in his appearance, came to see the goveronr. Murray, as usual, had a waiting room full of people, and the latest visitor took a seat at the end of the line.

When I learned he was C. N. Haskell, I sat down beside him. Thus began an acquaintance which ripened into a warm friendship during the remaining months of his life. In November, 1932, I was doing a historical series for the Oklahoma City Times and I wrote Haskell to ask that he relate his story of the removal of the capital.

"Yes, will help you all I can," was his reply, scrawled on the letterhead of the Turner hotel in Muskogee. It was one of two hand-written letters I received from Haskell, and the only one I have left; the other, unfortunately, was missing after I permitted the letters to circulate among guests at an after-dinner speech.

Haskell dictated his story to a stenographer at Muskogee, and it forms an integral part of the account of the capital removal in this volume.

After meeting Haskell, I decided to cultivate an acquaintance with the other former governors with the result that while I am only three years older than the State of Oklahoma, I have known personally every governor since statehood except Lee Cruce. I saw him only once, and that in the presidential campaign of 1928 when, a regular Democrat, as always, he introduced Al Smith at a rally in Oklahoma City.

From "Alfalfa Bill" Murray and his hefty bouncer, R. D. McManus, I heard day after day countless anecdotes of the "Con Con." McManus had been in Guthrie at the time of the Constitutional Convention, and what he lacked in scholarship he made up in first-hand knowledge of the foibles and personalities of the leading characters.

Those were hectic days at the capitol as the darkening gloom of the depression fell on Oklahoma and the nation. Beneath his rough exterior, Murray had a soft heart. I have seen hungry mothers with children come to the governor's office. McManus might steer some away, but it was not unusual for the governor to come storming from his inner office, streaming cigar smoke in his wake.

"What do you want?" he would thunder. The timid visitor might try to tell her troubles, only to be brushed aside; but as she left the office, McManus would overtake her to press a dollar or two from "Alfalfa Bill" into her trembling hand.

Our papers were hostile to Murray, at the outset; and he could be equally hostile. On three separate occasions, I was "kicked out" of press conference for some pointed question; but as time went on, the gruff old governor and I came to know each other better. Thus developed a friendship that covered a quarter of a century; and I am proud that, with the acquired background of past events, I could organize Squirrel Rifle Brigade No. 2 to honor "Alfalfa Bill" on his 80th birthday—Nov. 21, 1949—and to repay in small part the burdensome debt he had incurred personally to keep the Constitutional Convention members in Guthrie after the federal appropriation expired.

During his mellow moods, Murray would order hot water from the capitol cafeteria. When it arrived, he would reach into a lower drawer of his desk and pull forth a package of herbe mate—a South American tea. Then over a cup of steaming tea, Murray would lecture us on the Constitution, the New Deal, the llama—"the all-purpose animal of South America"—or any other of a myriad of subjects. Murray had few diversions; he used to say, "I don't deserve any credit for not gambling—I don't like to play cards." But I am sure he found relaxation from the press of duties in those sessions with the newsmen, for he remarks on them in his Memoirs:

"I recall with pleasure, while governor, such news reporters who were gentlemen so far as their editorial chiefs would permit them to be. They were: Charles Haslet, Associated Press reporter; Frank McNaughton, general reporter for the United Press, both in Washington now (1945).

"In addition there were Otis Sullivant, of the Oklahoman; Lee Hills of the Oklahoma and Times; Harold Mueller of the Oklahoma City Times; Parker LaMoore of the Oklahoman, and Lee Erhard of the Tulsa World.

"In this connection, I particularly desire to mention Irvin Hurst who, in the beginning, thought he did not like me, but became and is yet, one of my best friends."

From this acquaintance with Oklahoma's governors, it was only a step to an after-dinner speech on the governors which I have given in some 55 or 60 towns and cities in all sections of the state. Invariably, the talk would inspire reminiscences, and old timers would come up afterwards to relate personal experiences.

I remember one such occasion when I had addressed the Rotary club at Lindsay. A man of 70 years or more—and I regret that I did not write down his name—told me of a call on Haskell to collect for a wagon and harness sold to the new training school at Pauls Valley.

"I was in business then as a hardware merchant, and the bill came to about $250," he said. "The state had no money, and I carried the account as long as I could. One day I caught the train to Guthrie and went in to see the governor. I told him my predicament. Haskell got out his checkbook, wrote me a check for $250, and told me, 'When you get paid, you can repay me.'"

After 50 years, it is still difficult to get an accurate appraisal of Oklahoma's first governor. In his day, he was denounced as a political scoundrel and praised as a benevolent genius; but on one point, admirers and detractors are in general accord. Haskell was a man of tireless energy, daring and resourceful to the Nth degree.

I was dismayed when I began research on the Haskell administration to learn how little official correspondence is preserved. Haskell was a prolific letter writer and the newspapers of his day, while frequently partisan and unfriendly, were generous in publishing his letters and statements in full. This practice was fortunate in furthering an objective study of the controversial acts of his administration—and most of Haskell's acts provoked controversy. When I embarked on this project, I intended to cover 50 years from the opening of the Constitutional Convention on Nov. 20, 1906. But as I delved deeper into original sources, and my limited personal resources dwindled, I decided to end this volume with the removal of the capital.

That marked the end of the Guthrie era, and the advent of a new period. Later, I hope to carry the story forward through two World Wars, the collapse of the Depositors' Guaranty Fund, the Tulsa race riot, the impeachment sessions, and down to the present.

One word about the constitution: Over the years, I have known personally perhaps 200 legislators. In conducting a little informal poll, I have yet to find a lawmaker who has seen the original parchment copy. Sadder still, I am forced to suspect that few have read the constitution in any form!

Oklahoma has a rich historical heritage. It is unfortunate that the original constitution is not on display for lawmakers and the public, as is the United States constitution in the Library of Congress. The constitution directs that it shall be "sacredly preserved" by the secretary of state, but that doesn't mean it has to be tossed into an unsightly iron box with the dismantled original Great Seal of State and a pile of miscellaneous papers.

Put the constitution on display! And while about it, let's have a public reading of salient features for public officials. Much of Oklahoma's turmoil in government comes from a careless or wanton disregard of the plain provisions of the constitution and a virtual obliteration of the lines between the three separate and coordinate branches of government.

Like sugar, pepper and salt which are kept in separate containers, the constitution commands that "the legislative, executive and judical departments of government shall be separate and distinct, and neither shall exercise the powers properly belonging to the other." That is Article IV, the shortest in the constitution; it was inserted to provide the checks and balances so necessary in a republican form of government.

Over the years, the legislative has so encroached upon a supine executive department that the lawmakers have taken over in large part the functions of highway building, state purchases and state employment. Both in omission and in commission, Oklahoma's lawmakers sin daily against the constitution.

"The apportionment of this state for members of the legislature shall be made at the first session of the legislature after each decennial Federal census," reads Section 10-B of Article V. Could it be any clearer? It doesn't take a constitutional lawyer to interpret Section 18 of the same article, which created the legislative department. This section provides:

"No person shall serve as a member of the legislature who is, at the time of such service, an officer of the United States or state government, or is receiving compensation as such . . .," yet it is not uncommon to see a legislator serving in federal position, or taking compensation from a subdivision of government for which he votes appropriations!

How could the constitution be more specific than in Section 23 of Article V? It reads:

"No member of the legislature shall, during the term for which he was elected, be appointed or elected to any office or commission in the state, which shall have been created, or the emoluments of which shall have been increased, during his term of office, *nor shall any member receive any appointment from the governor, the governor and senate, or from the legislature, during the term for which he shall have been elected . . .*"

Yet the commission set up to sponsor observance of Oklahoma's 50 years of statehood is headed by a legislator, appointed by the governor; and that commission is empowered to spend some $275,000 of the people's money this year, with an additional $250,000 appropriation request pending. The constitution plainly intended that the three co-ordinate branches of government work in harmony, but not in collusion. Otherwise, the public is denied the benefit of checks and balances so necessary to preserve a healthy regard for the people's liberties and a wholesome respect for the dollars they pay in taxes.

The framers of Oklahoma's constitution spent just four days short of a year in perfecting that document and waging a bitter fight for statehood. The language of the constitution is not academic; it is "the fundamental law of the State of Oklahoma." A closer adherence to its provisions would make for a better government and for a greater Oklahoma.

Oklahoma City, Okla.,
March 16, 1957

Table of Contents

Illustrations

CHAPTER I

The 'Con Con' Days

JUNE 14, 1906, was a day of jubilation throughout Oklahoma and Indian territories. After years of "carpet bag" rule and frustrating efforts to win statehood, either as one state or as two, the promise of sovereignty was in sight. Before packed galleries, the house of representatives late in the afternoon completed work on the Enabling Act which would unite these two diverse territories and bring them into the Union as the forty-sixth state.

"Bill passed the house 5:23. Shake," read a telegram from Bird S. McGuire, Oklahoma territory's delegate in congress, to Frank Frantz, the appointive territorial governor in Guthrie. Two days later, President Theodore Roosevelt signed the act into law laying down the procedure for electing delegates to the Constitutional Convention and appropriating $100,000 for expenses of the convention.

Under the Enabling Act, each territory would elect 55 delegates to the convention, with two additional delegates from the Osage nation, and those 112 men would write the basic law for the new state of Oklahoma.

Some enthusiastic boosters were so optimistic as to predict statehood soon after the first of the new year. The combined population of the two territories was 1,414,000, as a special census would show, the largest number of inhabitants for any embryo state. Nevada had been admitted in 1864—when Abraham Lincoln partisans figured they might need some additional electoral votes to re-elect the Great Emancipator—with less than 30,000 citizens! Oklahoma's two territories embraced some 69,839 square miles of territory, with 5,200 miles of mainline railroads. There were 241 national banks and about twice that many other banks.

But the enthusiasts had failed to reckon with the vagaries of politics and the vexing problems of an Enabling Act which threatened to shackle the new commonwealth with inhibitions and concessions. The act provided that the capital should remain in Guthrie until 1913; the new state should extend prohibition over the Indian territory and Osage nation for 21 years, and the state must provide a republican (with little "r") form of government "without distinction" in civil or political rights. Previous similar acts had used the word "discrimination," but the choice of language carried a more restrictive meaning. And the state was required to grant tax exemptions on certain Indian lands.

"No state ever came into the Union more qualified in any respect for statehood than does Oklahoma," observed the great Senator Joseph W. Bailey of Texas, "yet Congress has put upon her the badge of incompetency by refusing to let her select her own capital and denying her the right to regulate her own affairs by forcing prohibition. Congressmen forced upon her not what Oklahoma herself wanted, but what other states wanted her to have."

Frank Frantz
Young Enid "Rough Rider" was Roosevelt's choice as governor.

These restrictions would prove galling during the months of travail, but the immediate outcry from Democratic politicians—once the shouting over the joys of approaching statehood had subsided—was over the reported "gerrymander" in carving out the delegate districts. That function had been left to commissions headed by Governor Frantz, in Oklahoma territory, and by W. H. H. Clayton, senior U. S. judge in Indian territory. Protests brought some revisions in district lines, but the charges of "gerrymander" would echo throughout the campaign for delegates.

At a Republican rally in Bartlesville on August 4, Frantz asserted: "I am for a Republican constitutional convention. The best men in the state, we believe, will be found in the Republican party." Democrats had directly opposite views. In Indian territory, men who had served in the Sequoyah convention at Muskogee the year before set their caps to dominate the new convention, and most of them were Democrats.

One of the foremost was dynamic Charles N. Haskell, 46-year-old native of Ohio, who had come to Muskogee as a railroad promoter only five years before. As vice president, Haskell was one of the moving lights in the Sequoyah convention which met August 21, 1905, to draft a constitution for the proposed State of Sequoyah. In fact, Haskell had inspired the call for the Sequoyah convention. Working first through his friend, General Pleasant Porter, principal chief of the Creek nation, and later with leaders of the other Five Civilized tribes, Haskell had prevailed on the Indians to call the convention. While Haskell had slight hopes for a separate state for Indian territory, he privately expressed the view that defeat in this effort would reconcile the Indian leaders to joint statehood with Oklahoma territory.

Also prominent in the Muskogee convention was another vice president, 36-year-old William H. Murray of Tishomingo, a farmer-lawyer who had married Alice Hearrell, a niece of Gov. Douglas H. Johnston of the Chickasaws. He served on the committee which actually drafted the Sequoyah constitution. Despite vociferous objections, particularly from lawyers, the Sequoyah constitution carried by large majority when submitted to the people of Indian territory; but separate statehood was doomed when Roosevelt flatly declared there should not be two states, but one, for Oklahoma. Events would prove, however, that experience at Muskogee would give the Indian territory delegates a decided advantage at Guthrie.

On August 24, 1906, Governor Frantz issued his proclamation for the election November 6, with the convention to open two weeks later. In an era when the railroads dominated the politics in many states, a spontaneous event was to have far-reaching effect on selections. Returning from seven months in Washington buttonholing congressmen to support the Enabling Act, Henry Asp was drafted by Guthrie Republicans as a delegate. Asp was highly respected by men of both parties, but since 1889 he had been attorney for the Santa Fe railroad in Guthrie and as a Republican candidate, he stood as a symbol of railroad influence that Democrats fanned into a flame of victory.

Republicans were aghast to see the Democrats sweep the election, with 98 delegates and one independent who joined the Democratic caucus. Haskell, while actually elected on a Greater Muskogee ticket, was recognized as a leader among the Democrats, bringing their number to 100. Two days after the election, the moderate *Oklahoma State Register* observed:

"The Democratic landslide . . . is so terrific it has taken the breath of the Republicans. The defeat of the Republican party is due to prohibition, lack of organization and the nomination of Henry Asp . . . Other railroad attorneys were nominated, but none were so conspicuous. None had a reputation for ability, and none struck the popular prejudice against railroad domination as he did. He was the issue everywhere—in Indian territory and Oklahoma—and cost the party thousands of votes away from home for the loyalty for him at home."

In fairness to Asp, it should be noted that both Murray and Haskell sang his praises in later years. Murray was to write in his Memoirs, "there was no man in the convention in whom I had more confidence in his word than Henry Asp . . . He was honorable, honest, upright, and really a great man. I say that, although he was the leading Republican in the convention and, in fact, one of the ablest in the convention."

Henry Asp
An able delegate, his railroad connections cost party dearly.

It was obvious the Democrats would organize the convention. The beehive of activity around the Turner hotel in Muskogee was even more portent. With 34 members of the old Sequoyah convention elected, C. N. Haskell held the trump cards. Murray, checking the list, noted an additional 30 members from the Farmers Union. He wrote Haskell:

"You will observe those marked with an 'S' means Sequoyah. Those marked 'F' means Farmer Union—64 in number. Do you know a man in western Oklahoma that would be fitted for the presidency?"

Summoned to Muskogee by long distance telephone, Murray conferred with Haskell and Robert L. Owen, part Cherokee and a brilliant lawyer, destined to become one of Oklahoma's first United States senators. The gaunt Murray, with handlebar mustache, might be eccentric, but he was a student of constitutional law; moreover, as a member of the Farmers Union, he had a strong following among farm delegates. He would do for president. Planning aloud, Haskell said he would take his "one wife" and go to Guthrie a week early. He advised Murray to come later. On his return home, Murray met George A. Henshaw at the railroad station in Madill. Henshaw, a delegate, volunteered his support.

"You can ruin me," said Henshaw, mindful of the coming battle to fix county lines, "but I trust to your gratitude." His trust would be rewarded in time with the formation of Marshall county with Madill as county seat, although only a bare 12 miles from Tishomingo.

The Royal hotel, still standing as a rooming house, was the political and social hub of Guthrie. When Haskell arrived and asked for a room, J. M. Brooks, the proprietor, told him they were "all taken for delegates to the convention." Checking the register, Haskell said he found the names of only five delegates, "the rest being lobbyists." Thereupon he determined upon a course to curb the lobbyists and it was adopted by the convention as resolution No. 1. Brooks finally found quarters for Haskell, and his room No. 47 became symbolic in street corner discussions in the months ahead.

Guthrie, designated as a land office site in 1889, had been capital of Oklahoma territory since passage of the Organic act to organize the territory in May, 1890. It was a thriving city of 12,000, with nine railroads and 42 passenger trains daily—an indication of the railroads' importance in the life of the community. It had two daily newspapers and a weekly. In the partisan spirit of a lusty age, the *Oklahoma State Capital* (Republican), edited by Frank Hilton Greer, and the *Leader* (Democratic), edited by Leslie G. Niblack, hurled invectives at each other and touted their partisan claims. The weekly *Register*, while Republican, followed a more temperate line under the revered John Golobie, a Czech immigrant who later served with distinction in the state senate.

Characteristic of the times was an item from Tishomingo, I. T., appearing in the *Leader* of Nov. 16, 1906. It reported a resolution by a "Democratic mass meeting" on November 14 indorsing William H. Murray for president of the convention. Murray was described as "a good parliamentarian, an impartial arbiter, a well-prepared constitutional lawyer, a politician too wise and too honorable to barter away his position by political promises, trades or intrigues."

It was signed by S. C. Treadwell, president, and E. C. Patton, secretary, but any one familiar with Murray's style could easily detect his modest authorship! Moreover, as he related the incident years later, Murray met Treadwell and Patton near the stairs leading to the second floor of the bank building and in sidewalk conversation, broke the news of his intentions to capture the presidency. The same day the *Leader* story appeared, Murray checked in at the Royal and began to greet other delegates, most of them strangers to him. Haskell continued his conferences in room 47. Adjacent to the hotel lobby on the west was a saloon, where delegates pondered the coming battle over prohibition and other problems; while a door to the east was the entrance to the Brooks opera house.

Speculation was rife over the presidency. W. C. Hughes, Oklahoma City, was an aspirant. So was Pete Hanraty of McAlester, one of the two foreign-born delegates. Henry S. Johnston of Perry was receptive.

By Monday, November 19, however, Haskell and Murray had their forces organized. In the Democratic caucus, only Murray and Hanraty were placed in nomination. Murray polled 62 votes to 26 for Hanraty, one being Murray's own vote. Johnston was chosen caucus chairman. The stage was set—literally—for the formal opening next day in the Brooks opera house.

Shortly after 2 p. m. on Tuesday, Johnston banged the gavel. So keen was the excitement, tickets had been allocated—three to a delegate —and the opera house was jammed. Joseph Francis King of Newkirk was chosen as temporary chairman, and the convention proceeded to elect permanent officers. Murray won over Philip B. Hopkins of Muskogee, the Republican favorite, 97 to 11, and immediately launched into his inaugural speech. In retrospect, it proved to be a blueprint for the constitution.

"We are now united, not as two territories, but as Greater Oklahoma," he asserted. Then in prophetic vein, he continued:

"First, let us make a constitution without the sting of partisanry, because the conditions of today may be reversed tomorrow and you may thus have to take the same dose yourself that you dosed out to your fellow citizens.

"The provisions of education should be liberal, and as near non-partisan as possible . . . A measure of vast importance will be to provide every possible means to promote home-owning in this country . . . If a few men, and great corporations, are to get control of the lands of the Indian in the Indian territory portion of the state, the removal of restrictions will not mean happiness and prosperity, but rather the reverse.

"Now the next evil. We must provide in the constitution that no public service corporation shall own any more land than that which shall be necessary to operate its business." This suggestion was a forerunner of the escheat provision.

Relative to labor, Murray proposed an 8-hour day, and any agreement between employee and employer exempting the latter from damages for death or injury should be declared null and void.

How far the state has progressed in race relations in half a century is revealed in Murray's suggestions for government attitude toward Negroes. The clamor for "Jim Crow" provisions requiring separate railroad coach and waiting room facilities was loud among the delegates. After indorsing this suggestion, he added:

"We have no desire to do the Negro an injustice. We shall protect him in his real rights . . . We must provide the means for the advancement of the Negro race and accept him as God gave him to us, and use him for the good of society. . . .

"He must be taught in the line of his own sphere as porters, bootblacks and barbers, and many lines of agriculture, horticulture and mechanics, in which he is adept. But it is an entirely false notion that the Negro can rise to the equal of the white man in the professions, or become an equal citizen to grapple with public questions . . ." Significantly, while Murray reprinted much of his inaugural address in his Memoirs, he omitted the section above.

The president also touched on the free pass evil of the day, suggesting a provision later incorporated in the oath for public office. Referring to passes as "the cheapest form of bribery," Murray declared: "We should say to every public officer that if he rides a free pass, he will also ride in stripes to the penitentiary!"

He declared for the initiative and referendum, then a "radical" theory, in operation in Switzerland and already adopted by the state of Oregon.

"The only argument ever offered against this system," he asserted, "is that the people are not conservative, while the history of the optional power is that the people are more conservative than reform leaders."

Summing up his recommendations, Murray concluded with this hope for the organic law "for the future state of Oklahoma:

That her fair form may stand and shine,
Make bright our days and light our dreams,
Turning to scorn with lips divine
The falsehood of extremes."

The opening session closed early, to clear the opera house for the night performance of the musical extravaganza, "It Happened in Norland."

The delegates held their first business session the next day, November 21, in the second floor convention quarters of the city hall, by singing "Nearer My God to Thee." It was President Murray's 37th birthday, but the anniversary apparently went unnoticed.

The *Register* reported, "the organization is all in the hands of Indian territory. C. N. Haskell is the power behind the throne." Regarding Murray, the paper observed, "he was not known in Guthrie prior to his appearance on the scene of statehood organization, and he gained instant favorable impression." The paper added, "he delights in the sobriquet, 'Alfalfa Bill.' " In succeeding months, he also would be dubbed "Cocklebur Bill" and worse epithets, but the name people would remember had come to light. "Alfalfa Bill" was edging into the limelight.

Some time later, the people had a box score on the delegates. They were natives of 17 different states and two foreign countries. Hanraty was born in Scotland and Joseph J. Curl of Bartlesville was a native of England. The oldest was "Uncle" Clem Rogers, 68. His son, Will, was then known as a globe-trotting cowhand. The youngest was William C. Liedtke, 24, from Eufaula. The average age: 43.

There were 47 farmers, 27 lawyers, 12 merchants, three newspapermen, three teachers, including J. S. Buchanan of the University of Oklahoma history faculty; six preachers, two doctors, and two listed their occupations as "investments." Among the miscellaneous callings were a civil engineer, a bookkeeper, and a miners' union official (Hanraty). Carlton Weaver was a student at the University. It was obvious the farmer-labor element was in control, and their influence would be reflected in the constitution's drastic provisions to regulate the corporations.

Texas was the native state of 17, and 12 came from Missouri, including J. H. Maxey of Shawnee who had served in the Missouri constitutional convention in 1875. Incidentally, his death a year later was the first among the delegates. A crosscheck showed 75 delegates native to the south, 33 from the north, and the two born abroad. The only native son of Virginia was J. H. N. Cobb of Sapulpa, a Republican. F. E. Herring of Elk City claimed oldest residence in Oklahoma territory. He was a member of Capt. David L. Payne's "Boomer" company that invaded the territory in 1887 only to be driven out by U. S. troops.

On one occasion, "Uncle Clem" Rogers broke the tension of a midnight session on county boundaries by observing, "it would have been a godsend to this convention if they hadn't sent so many lawyers here. If there hadn't been so many lawyers, there wouldn't have been all this cutting up over technicalities!"

The new was hardly worn off before the convention was locked in its first floor fight. When J. A. Baker of Wewoka, to comply with the

LEDBETTER SAYS U. S. CONSTITUTION IS NOT SUPREME

The Rights of the State of Oklahoma Will be Subordinate to Nothing, Says the Delegate From Ardmore—Springs the State Rights Question in the Convention—Called Down by Williams Who Said This is Playing Poor Politics—All the Doings Yesterday of the Constitution Makers

The constitution of the United States was adopted by the constitutional convention here today, but the words in the resolution presented by J. A. Baker declaring it to be the highest and the paramount law of the new state were eliminated after the most exciting debate of the two day's session.

W. A. Ledbetter of Ardmore, who opposed Mr. Baker's resolution declaring the constitution of the United States paramount in the new state, interjected a little sensation into the debate. He said:

"We should resist the encroachments of federal power here in this state. We have been wrongly limited in our powers by congress, and should assert our rights to enter the union on an equality with the other states. We must go into the union with our head bowed, and should go just as far as we must under the enabling act in recognizing the powers of the federal government and no farther. We should not put a future embargo on the state adopting a resolution

The first scrap in the convention, as reported in the Capital for Nov. 27, 1906.

Enabling Act, proposed the convention adopt a resolution declaring the constitution of the United States as "the highest and paramount law of Oklahoma," W. A. Ledbetter of Ardmore, objected vehemently.

"While it is our duty to comply with the Enabling Act, it is also our duty to resist the encroachment of the federal government upon the reserved rights of the state," he declared. The delegates sided with him. As finally written into Section 1 of Article I, the constitution proclaims Oklahoma "an inseparable part of the Federal Union, and the Constitution of the United States is the supreme law of the land."

The next scrap came over the preamble. When a committee came in with a proposed draft which began, "We, the people of the State of Oklahoma, wishing the guardianship of the Supreme Ruler of the Universe," the storm broke. Leave God out? mumbled the stunned delegates. Cobb, a minister, asked the committee members if their mothers taught them to use "Supreme Ruler of the Universe" in their prayers. The convention was operating in committee of the whole, with Johnston in the chair. Murray was on the floor.

"Damn it," said the president, in an aside remark, "you cannot leave God out of the constitution!" He got the proposed preamble referred to a special committee, and the next day he came in with a substitute which began, "Invoking the guidance of Almighty God." Lifted almost bodily from the Sequoyah constitution, it was readily adopted. For years, friends jokingly declared Murray "cussed God into the constitution," but he insisted the word "damn" is not swearing—and cited court decisions in support!

Hurricane clouds were gathering, meantime, over the county boundary committee. While county lines had been defined in various openings in Oklahoma territory, there were no counties in Indian territory. The nearest approach were recording districts, but they did not meet the requirements for counties. The problem was unique for a constitutional convention, but the tremendous pressure for local advantage threatened the main work of the delegates. Some 300 towns and cities were seeking county seats, and most of them had lobbyists in Guthrie—notwithstanding resolution No. 1.

Royal J. Allen, Duncan grocer, headed the committee, but the fight was more than he could cope with. Murray went to Don P. Wills, of Chelsea, one of the less aggressive members. If assured his county would be defined as he wished, would Wills step aside? He agreed, and Murray promptly named Haskell as a substitute. Determined to settle the disputes before the Christmas recess, Murray and Haskell plunged into night-long sessions with the committee. Finally, they whipped out a report defining 54 new counties. With 21 from old Oklahoma, that brought the total to 75. Feelings were tense on the convention floor, but Murray ignored delegates seeking to adjourn. Playing for time to permit Haskell to complete his report, the president encouraged Col. W. H. Moore of St. Louis, president of the Good Roads association, to talk on and on in the afternoon session of December 18 while the president kept an anxious eye on the door. When Haskell appeared with a handful of papers, Murray shouted, "the delegate from Muskogee is recognized," and Haskell came forward.

The descriptions were so complicated (comprising nearly 10,000 words in the constitution) that there had not been time to get them typed. Haskell was impressed as reading clerk, and delegates living 50 years later marvelled at his ability to give the boundaries from notes. Not all the new counties were in Indian territory. The "empire of Woods county" was carved into three—Woods, Alfalfa and Major—and a sprawling domain of 1,500,000 acres, Greer county, was divided, in painful surgery. Day county was dissolved and Grand, the county seat, eventually vanished from the map. David Hogg, the delegate from Grand, moved to name the new county Ellis, for A. H. Ellis of Orlando, the second vice president of the convention.

When Haskell reached Section 20 of the report, he noticed a difference of opinion over the name. He moved to substitute "Hughes," for W. C. Hughes, "to honor one of the foremost citizens of Oklahoma." A few minutes later, Boone Williams of Lehigh moved to name Section 22 for Haskell. "There is no county in the new state," Haskell prophesied, "wherein the farmer will prosper more than he will in the county named in my honor." Alfalfa and Murray were named for Murray, Latimer for Delegate J. S. Latimer, and Bartlesville was changed to Washington, at Curl's suggestion. Coo-wees-coo-wee (as suggested by Clem Rogers) was fortunately changed to Rogers. "Uncle" Clem beamed with gratitude. McClain and Major were named for Delegates Charles M. McClain, Purcell, and J. C. Major, Fairview; Harper for O. G. Harper, a clerk in the convention. (See appendix for how the counties got their names).

In a night session December 21, the convention reached roll call on the Haskell report. "Every Republican voted against us but J. H. N. Cobb of Sapulpa," Murray wrote in his Memoirs. When Cobb voted "yes," he received a friendly nod from the president—and thus Sapulpa became county seat, instead of Bristow! Incidentally, the county's name was changed from Moman— for Moman Pruiett, the noted criminal lawyer—to Creek, for the Indian tribe, after the holidays. Pruiett, supporting Lee Cruce, Ardmore banker, as prospective candidate for governor, had offended Haskell.

Thus it is that while the counties are listed alphabetically in the

*The Capital's uncomplimentary view of county boundaries.**

*The cartoonist was Win Fazel, son of a Methodist missionary then living in Guthrie. C. M. Sarchet of Ponca City, then city editor of the *Capital*, said Fazel "was a young fellow, perhaps this was his first regular employment. The Fazels left Guthrie some time afterward and located in Topeka. The boy was good, and must have gone on up from there." Working with chalk plates, the cartoonist etched his drawings into the soft chalk from which the cuts were cast for publication.

constitution, Creek comes between Mayes and Murray—where Moman normally would have appeared!

Of the 75 counties, Haskell pointed out, 37 were in Indian territory, 35 in Oklahoma territory, and three straddled the line. Still the division left political sores that began to fester. As the weary delegates departed for home and the holidays, a new cry of "gerrymander" went up throughout the territories, this time from the Republican newspapers.

As the delegates settled down to business early in December, a young man went on trial at Herkimer, N. Y., for the murder of his pregnant sweetheart. He was Chester Gillette. The body of the girl, Grace Brown, had been found in the waters of Big Moose in the Adirondacks the preceding July. Gillette went to the electric chair March 30, 1908, but Theodore Dreiser would take the elements of this true-life drama and weave them into a best-seller novel *An American Tragedy*.

And early in 1907, wealthy Harry K. Thaw would go on trial for the murder of Stanford White, the noted architect, in New York. It was a period when killings to avenge marital "wrongs" were common, and crime news filled a good portion of the daily newspapers which the delegates read.

During the holidays, there was an outbreak of smallpox among the prisoners in the city jail, in the basement of the convention hall. When the delegates reconvened, "Uncle" Clem Rogers and Johnston fell victims to the disease and were quarantined in their rooms for a couple of weeks. Mrs. Haskell helped look after the sick.

Six weeks were gone, but the main task lay ahead when the delegates reconvened Jan. 3, 1907. What about the railroads? the corporations? woman's suffrage? Jim Crow? prohibition? All were troublesome problems, and all must be faced in writing the basic law. Lobbyists thronged the hotel lobby, and filled the assembly balconies. Already, there were hints that Teddy Roosevelt was displeased. Pay, under the congressional appropriation, would stop January 24, and there had been no response from Washington to overtures for more money.

Prohibition came first. Under the Enabling Act, it was mandatory in the Indian territory for 21 years. Rev. E. C. Dinwiddie of Washington, D. C., headed the active prohibition lobby. The convention *had* to write prohibition into the constitution for part of the state; Haskell, flirting with the prohibitionists in anticipation of the race for governor, advocated going a step farther. He declared he was against a "calico constitution," with one law for one section and a different law for other parts of the state. The upshot was a provision in the constitution extending the 21-year rule for Indian territory and a separate ordinance, to be submitted to popular vote with the constitution, making prohibition statewide.

Next came the suffrage question. Sentiment appeared to favor woman suffrage until Guthrie held a school election. With indorsement from the Farmers Union, American Federation of Labor and railroad organizations, the advocates of woman suffrage claimed pledges from 67 delegates. Robert L. Owen was on hand to support their cause.

Debate swelled into battle on the floor February 5 when Hanraty moved to strike "male" from the section defining qualified electors. Women thronged the galleries. Only four states—Colorado, Idaho, Utah and Wyoming—had given women the ballot. Would Oklahoma be the fifth? Those opposing argued that "good" women wouldn't vote. When Hogg, a widower, declared, "they don't want to vote—the majority of them," there was a woman's voice from the gallery. "Yes, I do, Mr. Hogg. I want to vote the worst kind."

The chairman banged for order, and Haskell took the floor. He quoted liberally from the Bible and pictured his listeners coming home "to find a candidate for county commissioner has taken so much of your wife's time that it really hadn't occurred to her that supper was a part of every day life."

Murray credited Mrs. Haskell with helping form her husband's decision to oppose woman suffrage. When Haskell had said at Muskogee, "I'll take my one wife and go to Guthrie a week early," he was giving humorous expression to a situation well-known among Haskell's acquaintances. The remark produced a ripple of smiles, for all were aware how inseparable were Haskell and his wife.

During the campaign for governor, later, Mrs. Haskell was present for all but two of her husband's meetings. When he became governor, it was a familiar sight for visitors to find Mrs. Haskell knitting in her husband's outer office. Friends said she was a keen judge of character, and not adverse to expressing her opinions. Moreover, Haskell listened.

"At the time that Robert Owen was striving to adopt woman's suffrage, I was in Haskell's apartment talking to him, Mrs. Haskell being present," Murray related in his Memoirs. "Owen came in and asked Haskell how he stood. Haskell said, 'I haven't made up my mind yet.'

"Mrs. Haskell, who really was his mentor, spoke up immediately and said, 'I know how he is; he will be against it.' Owen asked her why. Mrs. Haskell said:

" 'Women vote for love or hate; that is the thing that moves them. They have got to do it in self defense.' Well, he rather denied that, and she said: 'I will give an example. I had an old teacher that was very strict and he made me study, as he ought to, but I hated him. After he retired from the profession, he ran in that town in Ohio for school trustee, and a saloon bum ran against him. I voted for the saloon bum.' "

Henry Asp got into the argument. "I don't believe that giving woman the right to vote means you are going to unsex her," he asserted. There was a modest gasp from the galleries, then a murmur of approval. "The women may not vote," he added, "but their right to vote will be held over the heads of nominating conventions in Oklahoma, and they will nominate clean men."

The Hanraty motion was tabled, 57 to 28, with Murray, Haskell and R. L. Williams among those in the majority. Privately, the delegates revealed later the school election had increased the opposition. From convention hall, the delegates could see the polling place where Negroes had been in preponderance among the women voters. Six weeks later, by one-vote margin, the convention did make a concession to women folk by extending to them the right to vote in school elections only.

Jim Crow—the term apparently originated in southern states from a character in a minstrel show—still inspired speeches so inflammatory it is difficult to realize the extent of race prejudice 50 years ago. Left on their own, the delegates would have voted separate school and travel facilities overwhelmingly. But Frantz dropped the hint in a speech that President Roosevelt would reject the constitution if racial discrimination features were adopted; the Enabling Act, it was noted, had forbidden "distinction" in civil rights. Under Haskell's counsel, the convention rejected the separate coach proposition, 46 to 31, on February 27. Then it promptly adopted a Haskell resolution recommending that the legislature "do, by law, require railroads to provide separate but equal coaches," adding that "we consider this a legislative, rather than a constitutional, question."

"Statehood," Haskell argued, "is the all-important question."

Eleven statewide elective offices had been created, including the office of clerk of the state supreme court, when the insurance committee reported in early March. The report provided for an appointive commissioner. Up jumped R. L. Williams with a substitute motion to elect the official.

Chairman McClain of Purcell, an insurance man, insisted "the best way to get a competent man is to have him appointed." "Nonsense," cried Haskell. Murray, supporting the committee, lost 52 to 33—and thus Oklahoma elects 12 constitutional officers statewide—and since the first election, the primary ballot has been a windfall for trick names. In the first primary, a genial salesman born William M. Cross, a native of Tennessee, ran as Bill Cross for secretary of state, and in the intervening years every primary sees a crop of trick filings—from Willie Cornelius Rogers, shortened to Will, to Cowboy Pink Williams, born James Pinckney Williams. The former went to congress 10 years in statewide election; the latter became lieutenant governor.

"The people were tired of appointive officers," Murray wrote years later. "Some members of the convention, I verily believe, favored the election of national bank presidents by direct vote of the people. These errors were caused by pure demagoguery of some of the leaders."

With only five opposing, the convention adopted the initiative and referendum March 4. Patterned after the Oregon law, it was offered by Johnston in Article V setting up the legislative department. (Incidentally, the first seven measures submitted to the voters failed; the first adopted, June 11, 1910, moved the capital from Guthrie to Oklahoma City.)

CHAPTER II

A Contemporary Word Picture

ONE of the best word pictures of the convention came from Frederick Upham Adams who visited the session in which the initiative and referendum was adopted. Writing in *The Saturday Evening Post* the day Oklahoma became a state, Adams observed:

"It was about a year ago that Oklahoma was so sure of statehood that the delegates to draft a constitution were getting together in Guthrie . . . The city hall at Guthrie will be known for all time as the birthplace of the Oklahoma constitution, and we look forward to a day when children ten generations remote will stand with uncovered heads and gaze about the crumbling interior* of the room in which their inspired forefathers penned the immortal document which bequeathed them all of their wonderful prosperity. Doubtless there will be handed down to them tales of the ridicule and obliquy which were heaped on those pioneers who dared to build a ship of state with turbine engines instead of masts and sails, and they doubtless will believe that all of the wisdom perished with the men who happened to draft the constitution.

"Since we must worship something, constitutions serve most admirably. Surely there will be a marble statue to the Honorable William H. Murray, chairman of the Constitutional Convention, and conspicuous as one of its founders. There is no figure in revolutionary days more picturesque than Bill Murray, as his constitutents affectionally call him.

"He is the most handsome man in the state which has the right to boast of its men. He is a 'Squaw' man with a dash of Indian blood in his own veins, enough to give his straight figure a certain lithe grace and to lend black luster to his locks. He is a man of wealth, as men are rated in Oklahoma, and you would pick him out of a crowd and make no mistake in esteeming him one of the natural leaders of men.

"How the school histories of 2107 will be thumbed on pages which picture the Oklahoma Constitutional Convention in 1906-07! The chil-

*Unfortunately, the convention hall was razed in 1955.

dren will read of a time when railroads and trusts were all powerful in the United States. There will be held up to them a story of how tens of thousands of their impoverished ancestors were massed on the Cherokee line that memorable noon hour of the 22nd of April, 1889, when at the signal of the crack of cavalry carbines the land-hungry horde swept over the border and founded a commonwealth in a day.

"The children of the future will see Guthrie, Oklahoma City and other great municipalities rise in a night and they will thrill at the tale of the struggles of their forefathers against the combined terrors of the wilderness and the exactions of grasping, merciless and tyrannical corporations. Certain railroad names now familiar to Wall Street will probably have the same significance to the school children of 2107 as do the names of George III and Benedict Arnold to the peoples of today.

"The story of the Constitutional Convention will not suffer by comparison with the gatherings which we now reverence. It was not merely the birth of a new state; it was the birth of a new kind of state. Its founders claim that it is the first real democracy, the pioneer in the experiment of a true form of republican government. Its detractors assert that the visionaries and radicals from all other states poured into Oklahoma, and that the more rabid of them met and consolidated their theories into a hodge-podge which is certain to result in ever-lasting ruin; but I am of the opinion that it will take more than a freak constitution to hold Oklahoma back. She has done very well without any constitution, and I regret that she didn't try the experiment of continually doing without one. However, that is outside the subject.

"Let me contribute one picture for the future school-book historian. Scene, Guthrie; time, the spring of 1907; location, the city hall, from the tower of which one can look out on the sea of undulating hills and prairies, checkerboarded with fields of cotton and corn, and dotted to the horizon with herds of cattle. Within the hall I met the stalwart farmers who are forming the new constitution. Hovering about them are the lawyers and lobbyists who are there to represent the corporations and the 'vested interests.'

"It is only a resetting of the world-old picture of the battle of the masses against fortified power, save that the latter has been stripped of the weapons of force.

"The delegates are gathering. It is a day when there shall be decided the question of whether the 'initiative and referendum' be incorporated in the constitution. There are rumors that money has been

The "Con Con" in session, with Murray presiding. Ha
is man in front, hands on lap. Mrs. Haskell and friends

—OKLAHOMA HISTORICAL SOCIETY

HENRY S. JOHNSTON
As caucus chairman, he formally opened convention.

—PHOTO BY AUTHO

Room 47 (Bay Window). Royal hotel is now the Avon, a rooming house.

UNFOLD
DO NOT TEAR

ıor by the widow of Delegate John B. Harrison, later chief justice of the
town and party, see Appendix I.

This well-preserved composite picture of the 112 delegates was lent the au
State Supreme court. For further identification of the delegates by district

—OKLAHOMA HISTORICAL SOCIETY

:ell is third from front, in second row; Charles M. McClain, Purcell,
n balcony.

—MRS. JOHN B. HARRISON

The Convention hall—razed in 1955

—OKLAHOMA HISTORICAL SO

WILLIAM H. MURRAY
He observed 37th birthday day
convention opened.

used to advantage with delegates pledged for this radical reform. Excited farmers discuss this possibility and glare at the well-groomed attorneys who are arguing with the delegates.

"Chairman Bill Murray mounts the platform and sweeps the hall with his piercing glance. Down comes his gavel with repeated crashes on the table. The tumult ceases.

" 'The convention will come to order!' Murray shouts, with a final blow of the gavel. 'Delegates will take their seats, loafers and lobbyists will get out! We will begin by singing that grand old hymn, 'Nearer, My God, to Thee.' And as every delegate rises to his feet, the powerful voice of the chairman rings out to the words which all know and sing * * *

"If an attempt was made to use money to sway the votes of the men who met in Guthrie, it had as little effect as it would on Cromwell's Convenanters. The only human document of which they stood in awe was the constitution of the United States, and the only human being who influenced their decisions was President Roosevelt, the reason for which I shall explain later. The lobbyist is out of his depth in a place where men open their proceedings with 'Nearer, My God, to Thee,' and scores of times when the Oklahoma delegates met in Guthrie hall, its walls shook with the chorus of men who attempted to vote as they sang. * * *

"Now that it is all over, and the President has signed a proclamation which was mandatory and a mere formality, I violate no confidence in saying that the lawyers and corporation officials who journeyed to Washington and importuned Attorney General Bonaparte and President Roosevelt to thwart the wishes of the overwhelming majority of the most distinctively American community in the United States would have saved themselves a heritage of trouble by staying home. It is as easy to amend the Oklahoma constitution as it is to get signatures to a prohibition petition in a Methodist church, and the clauses stricken out will be re-inserted with new and sharper sets of teeth.

"A line between the 'masses' and the 'classes' was sharply drawn. The corporate interests campaigned and voted against the constitution and for the Republican ticket; the Democrats and Populists combined and voted for the constitution and the ticket headed by C. N. Haskell, the fusion candidate for governor. The result was an overwhelming victory for the constitutionalists and the Democratic-Populist allies. * * *

"The Oklahoma constitution is an attempt to grasp from the judiciary the power which it has either usurped or been permitted to absorb through the combined weakness and venality of the legislative branches. They will tell you in Oklahoma, and in other sections, that the courts are prone to declare unconstitutional any law aimed at the control of the corporations. Oklahoma proposes as a remedy that all such laws shall become a part of the constitution, and she is in a fair way to settle the mooted question of whether a constitution is constitutional."

While the portions quoted went far beyond the current action, Adams' analysis helps to keep the struggle in focus.

On March 5, Asp offered the Republican version of a "fair" constitution. It was a document of 135 pages bound in red. Among other notable provisions, it called for a senate of 25 members and a house of 50 members. Democrats noting the color of the binding promptly dubbed Asp's proposition the "red-light constitution," and otherwise ignored it. Asp, in turn, called attention to the yellow binding on the Democrats' printed sections and referred to their constitution as "the yellow peril." The exchange of puns enlivened the daily sessions remaining.

In mid-March, the convention was hurrying to what members hoped would be a close. On the thirteenth, they adopted the Schedule, prepared by Sam W. Hayes of Chickasha, for orderly transition from territorial status to statehood. Passing an ordinance for submitting the constitution to the voters on August 6, the convention went farther and created a "supreme election board" to conduct the canvass. They recessed then, on March 16, for a month to permit Murray and a committee to supervise copying on parchment the completed constitution for final adoption and signatures.

Ten days later, the storm broke over county divisions. Suit was filed for Greer county to enjoin the supreme election board from holding the August 6 election. Next day, March 27, H. A. Noah of Alva sued to enjoin submission of the constitution dividing Woods county. That same day, following a meeting of the Democratic central committee in Tulsa, Haskell announced for governor.

In an oral opinion April 9, Chief Justice C. H. Burford of the territorial supreme court, in his individual capacity as district judge at Guthrie, held for the convention on the issue of dividing counties. That, he said, was a legislative prerogative. But while the Enabling Act called for an election ordinance, Burford ruled the convention went too far in creating an election board. The election commission headed by the governor should function, he said.

C. N. HASKELL, EDITOR

C. A. LOONEY, ASSOCIATE EDITOR

New-State Tribune

NATIONAL SEALS

FIRST SETTLERS INDIAN TERRITORY

MUSKOGEE, IND. TER.,

March 17th 1907

Hon. Henry S. Johson:

Perry, O.T.

My dear Johnson:

I expected to get at least one more hand shake and a few words with you, before we parted last Friday, but in the mix up we got separated and I missed that pleasure. I also hoped to have another talk with your friend, but missed that pleasure also.

I am still in the same uncertain frame of mind that I was during the several days that we discussed the subject. There is, as a natural result of being among my friends and neighbors, a considerable demand that I enter the race for Governor and upon this subject I am still undecided. I sincerely meant what I said to you a time or two, viz, that I had no personal ambition to hold office for the mere distinction thereof; that the only inducement that would influence me in that direction, would be, First-- My pride in our grand new Constitution and my anxiety to see the mass of the people of this state enjoy the blessings of having, not merely the strict letter, but the full spirit of that Constitution carried into effect, and to insure this, I sincerely hope that our state officers, the Governor included, and our legislature, may all be men who are in strictest sympathy with this Constitution from a standpoint of honest sentiment and not solely because they may realize that pretended approval of the Constitution is necessary for them to deceive the Democracy of this State into nominating them. You know that so far as my acquaintance goes with Mr. Doyle, which has been limited to the time of the convention and his welcome visits thereto, that I consider him as having been a great aid in the Convention and believe that he is in sympathy with its work. I only regret that I am not sufficiently acquainted with the sentiment of the state to know whether the mass of the people are acquainted with him and to know what seems to be the spirit of a worthy leader.

The fact is, Johnson, I do not know what to do. I want to see the first administration of the State of Oklahoma, set the precedence of strict enforcement of our constitution to the end that we may begin aright, and our people may enjoy the blessings of honest government. I may be mistaken of the purposes of other candidates from my limited acquaintance with them, but I do have honest doubts of some, although I hope I am mistaken.

Please remember me kindly to Tom Doyle and my old Putnam County friend, Gust Kehres, and believe me,

Affectionately yours,

C N Haskell

Ten days before announcing for governor, Haskell was wooing Henry S. Johnston, a close friend of Thomas H. Doyle, also of Perry.

When the convention reconvened April 16, Haskell received an ovation. The day following, the convention—on Haskell's motion—adopted the mandatory primary provision. On April 18, by unanimous consent, the delegates suspended the rules to repeal the supreme election board feature.

Reading from the sheepskin parchment copy—the one which under its own terms is to be "sacredly preserved" by the secretary of state—the clerks embarked on a marathon reading session that Thursday night, with formal signing set the next day. It required about 18 hours to complete the reading. At 2:30 p. m., April 19, President Murray called the roll. Eighty-five answered "aye" for adoption, with 27 not voting.

Proudly, President Murray took a quill pen made from the feather of an eagle captured in Kay county and a stem of alfalfa from his farm to write "Wm. H." at 2:46 p. m. He finished his signature with a pen furnished by William J. Bryan, the idol of the Democrats, and under a resolution offered by Haskell, that pen was forwarded to Samuel Gompers, president of the American Federation of Labor. The quill pen went to the Oklahoma Historical Society.

John B. Harrison of Sayre, waiting to sign, observed the date was the anniversary of the "shot heard" round the world" at Concord. With Haskell booked to debate Thomas H. Doyle of Perry in the governor's race at Oklahoma City that night, some 60 delegates hurried to depart with him by special train. Both Muskogee delegates, Haskell and Hopkins, were permitted to sign out of order.

Murray draws cartoonist's fire.

Three days later, the convention by "ordinance irrevocable" accepted the Enabling

Act and the delegates took sentimental leave, formally recessing to the day before the August 6 election. Murray choked up, in delivering his farewell, and while tears dimmed the president's eyes, Johnston read the final remarks for him.

But instead of filing the original parchment copy with Charles H. Filson, territorial secretary of state, "Alfalfa Bill" put it in a strongbox and carried it back to Tishomingo. A howl went up from Republican papers about the "sight unseen" constitution. Governor Frantz refused to sign an election proclamation until the original document was on file. Although Murray later offered a "copy"—one of six typed versions—the

THE WEEKLY OKLAHOMA STATE CAPITAL SATURDAY, JUNE 8, 1907.

ALL ABOARD

The Capital *enlists recruits to oppose the constitution.*

governor stood firm again a proclamation without the original.

The impasse had its lighter moments when the witty Walter Ferguson, son of former territorial Gov. T. B. Ferguson, organized the Squirrel Rifle Brigade to "protect' the constitution. Murray was designated "general" and commander-in-chief. Commissions, bearing a grotesque picture of Murray, long flint-lock rifle in hand, with a cocklebur seal, became much-sought-after mementoes of the political crisis.

More serious conflicts were brewing. From a group of Oklahoma Republicans (Frank Greer of the *Capital* and Henry Asp among them) in Washington for conferences with Roosevelt came rumors that the president was displeased with many features of the constitution. Judge John L. Pancoast of Alva, one of the seven district judges making up the territorial supreme court, issued an injunction against Frantz calling the election. Some delegates were aghast at Murray's next move. Contending a constitutional convention beyond judicial reach, the "con con" president ignored Judge Pancoast's order and issued his own proclamation on June 3 for the election August 6. He called upon citizens of the two territories to finance it through contributions.

Finally, a committee of lawyers was formed to seek dissolution of Pancoast's order. Meantime, still another committee—Delegates Ledbetter, Hayes and Charles L. Moore of Enid—was sent to Washington to get Roosevelt's views on the constitution first hand. They were received at the White House, but later referred to Charles J. Bonaparte, the attorney general, for specific objections.

The campaign for the preferential primary sponsored by the Democratic central committee was coming to a climax. Although Haskell and Cruce both came from the Indian territory, it was obvious Tom Doyle, the only Oklahoma territory entry, would run a poor third as the former two engaged in a bitter battle. In the June 8 primary, Haskell was credited with 51,676 votes to Cruce's 48,206. Doyle's vote stood at 8,820. Although United States senate candidates were voted on statewide, Haskell had sponsored at the central committee meeting at Tulsa in March a "gentlemen's agreement" that one senator should come from the Indian territory side, the other from Oklahoma territory.

Robert L. Owen led the field, with 48,885. Second was Henry M. Furman of Ada, 39,113, but since both Owen and Furman came from the Indian territory, blind Tom P. Gore of Lawton, with 38,288, was

---

Remember the first scrap? The Capital revives the issue. ⟶

DECEMBER 1906

MAY 21, 1907

destined to become the senator from Oklahoma territory. Formal election would rest with the first legislature, however.

With the primary vote tabulated, Democrats met in state convention in Oklahoma City on June 18 to ratify the nominations. Murray presided and Bryan, back from a world tour, was a featured speaker. Cheers greeted the Great Commoner's compliments.

"You have the best constitution today of any state in the Union, and a better constitution than the constitution of the United States," he declared. "This is not extravagant praise. All the other states have stood as your models. I want to compliment the cornfield lawyers* of Oklahoma . . . upon having puttied up all the holes shot in the constitutions of other states by trust and corporation lawyers."

The Democrats pitched their campaign squarely on adoption of the constitution, declaring in their platform:

"We submit to the people of Oklahoma the best state constitution that has ever been written and in asking the suffrage of the patriotic citizenship of this state, we stand firmly on this constitution in its entirety as our platform."

On June 24, the territorial supreme court, 5 to 2, sustained Murray's contentions. "The power vested in the convention to form a state government implies the power to create and define all the counties within limits of the proposed state," wrote Justice E. F. Hainer for the majority. In the flush of victory, Murray dashed off a 2,000-word letter to Roosevelt asking the president to outline suggested changes.

Murray cited limitations of the Enabling Act on exempting certain lands from taxation, locating the capital at Guthrie, and the formation of five congressional districts by congress, then added:

"It is not our purpose to complain of the restrictions and limitations. We have accepted them in good faith. While we do not yield the point that a state in the exercise of its police powers or in the adoption of its economic policies, is either expected or required to frame a constitution to suit either the executive or legislative branches of the United States, yet in view of the uncertainties of statehood, which have wrought injuries to the business interests of the state, and in view of your authority under the Enabling Act . . . I, as president of the Constitutional Convention, respectfully request and solicit from you, an expression upon the constitution . . . and thus give us an opportunity to eliminate any provisions which will be necessary to secure executive approval. . . .

*A term applied previously somewhat derisively by the New York Herald-Tribune.

"I assure you that our citizens are committed to statehood as of first importance, and that party success or party advantage sinks into insignificance with all classes in comparison with the one thing, statehood now and without further delay * * *"

"It is human to err," he wrote, tongue in cheek. "We are prone to make mistakes and shall be glad to accept your superior counsel and advice in the spirit in which I am sure it would be given."

The letter had not been made public when Ledbetter, Hayes and Moore returned from Washington. It was obvious from their report, however, that the constitution must undergo extensive revision, and Murray asked the delegates to reconvene on July 10. As the delegates arrived, they were hurried to room 47 where Haskell—now the recognized leader of Oklahoma Democrats—briefed his followers. When

The July conferences in Room 47—as seen by the Capital.

Murray's letter to Roosevelt was read to the convention, the Democrats applauded. There was scattered applause from the Republicans for the one-sentence reply from the president's secretary, William Loeb, jr.

"Your letter of June 26th instant concerning the constitution of the proposed state of Oklahoma has been received by the president and the president has laid it before the attorney general," he wrote. So Roosevelt had refused to take the bait to engage in controversy with Murray.

R. L. Williams moved to recess the convention and Johnston promptly asked all but the Democratic delegates to leave. The Democrats remained in caucus most of the night. The next day, they offered 14 amendments. With unanimous consent to suspend the rules, they hurriedly acted to reconsider the vote by which the document had been adopted April 19. Then Ledbetter arose with typewritten copies of the amendments.

"As the proposed changes were read, the chair called for the roll call, and the votes were recorded, no explanation being given," the *Capital* reported. Angrily, Hopkins, the Republican leader, took the floor to denounce the action "without open discussion," but the Democratic machine rolled on. Rather than lose time recopying the parchment pages the leaders decided to enter the changes by interlineations. Words and phrases were inked out, the substitutes written in, and if the penmanship varies, it is because delegates and clerks lent a hand in recording the revisions.

The Capital pans secret sessions.

In four days, some 43 changes were made. One of the major revisions was in the article on the initiative and referendum. As written originally, it empowered the governor to write the rules by executive order if the legislature failed to make provision for vitalizing the section. That provision,

Ledbetter counseled, "is clearly unrepublican in form, and dangerous to approval by the president."

The controversial Article IX on corporations also was overhauled. A provision which would have prohibited foreign (out-of-state) corporations from petitioning for removal to federal court litigation filed in state courts, without consent of the opposing party, was stricken. Powers of the legislature "to discriminate against any foreign corporation" were modified to permit the legislature "to impose conditions" for licensing.

There was another concession to the women. In addition to serving as notary public, they were made eligible also to serve as county superintendent of schools. That's added, incidentally, in Hayes' handwriting. And, yielding to the clamor over "gerrymander" of legislative districts, the convention increased the house membership from 105 to 109, and the number of state senators from 41 to 44. The reapportionment section was hastily prepared in Spencerian script by C. C. Clothier, a bookkeeper at the ice plant who previously had prepared the lengthy county boundary descriptions. As the gavel fell on a "closing session" for the second time, there were feeble efforts to sing "God Be With You Till We Meet Again," but the words were lost in confusion. "In two minutes," the *Capital* reported, "the hall was deserted."

The official report for the special census of 1907 showed these classifications:

	Total Pop.	White	Negro	Indian	Mong.	Male	Female
Oklahoma Territory	733,062	688,418	31,511	13,087	46	390,232	342,830
Indian Territory	681,115	538,512	80,649	61,925	29	362.170	318,945
	1,414,177	1,226,430	112,160	75,012	75*	752,402	661,775

* Included four Japanese in Oklahoma territory, two in Indian territory.

Frantz opened his campaign for governor at Ada on Saturday, July 20. Striking at the Democrats' secret caucus sessions, the "rough rider" declared that "although they have a majority of 100 to 12 in the convention, they were afraid of the light of day." The Republican party, he asserted, "was the original statehood party. The Democrats of Oklahoma and Indian territories, as well as in congress, have always been obstructionists. . . ."

The *Capital,* meantime had installed a two-color press and now red headlines blazed across the front page. In daily cartoons, the Republican paper lambasted "Boss" Haskell and "Cocklebur" Murray. In a cartoon July 23rd, it depicted Washington, Hamilton and Jefferson in statues, towering over Murray and Haskell at a table below. "The Con Con was 240 days doing what our forefathers did in 85 days," read the caption. Jefferson did not serve in the convention which wrote the federal constitution, but what's historical accuracy in a partisan battle?

Murray was now ready to file the original document with Filson. Calling the territorial secretary of state from his hotel, Murray arranged an appointment. Accompanied by newsmen, and in jocular mood, "Alfalfa Bill" deposited the parchment copy, bound in red leather, in Filson's office at 3:46 p. m. It's the one which the secretary of state, charged with the duty "sacredly" to preserve, keeps in a heavy steel box.

"Immediately, citizens began to pour in to the secretary's office to see the parchment over which there has been so much discussion the past few months," the *Capital* related. "Each page of the document was scanned and the interlineations and varied penmanship noted."

Two days later, July 24, Frantz issued his proclamation setting the election for September 17—to coincide in date with adoption of the federal constitution. In Chicago, about the same time, Judge Kennesaw Mountain Landis in federal court handed down his famous decision in the Standard Oil rebate case, levying a record fine of $29,240,000 against the Rockefeller interests. Teddy Roosevelt's trust-busting efforts were bearing fruit.

The daily barrage continues.

But Oklahoma Republicans were in a quandary. The Democrats had pitched their campaign on the constitution. Meeting in Tulsa August 1, the Republicans nominated

Frantz by acclamation then straddled on the constitution.

"In the event that this partisan constitution shall become the fundamental law of the state, we pledge the Republican party . . . to use every means at their command to secure the speedy elimination of its objectionable features," read the platform. "On the other hand, if the judgment of the voters . . . shall be against this proposed constitution, or it shall be disapproved by the peerless Roosevelt, we assure the people that the Republicans of the two territories . . . will exert their power to have the coming congress . . . pass a new enabling act . . . under which a constitution and state government may be formed free from partisan bias and fair alike to all persons, interests and localities."

William Howard Taft, secretary of war, looming as leading Republican contender for the presidency in 1908, was brought to Oklahoma August 24 to fire salvos at the constitution.

"I don't think it is possible to amend it in such a way as to correct its defects," he asserted at Convention hall in Oklahoma City. "It needs complete revision. I wouldn't do it, because I should be confident that there would be a new enabling act if you rejected this constitution."

Whereupon the Democrats brought Bryan back on September 5.

"Adopt the constitution now," he thundered, speaking in the same hall, "because it is the best constitution in the United States . . . If you will read your constitution through, you will find it is full of the corrections made necessary by the experience of other states.

"Your constitution is easily amended . . . Why, my friends, the Democratic members of the constitutional convention made amendments so easy that even the Republican party in Oklahoma has enough votes to propose any amendment it wants!"

The battle was on. Murray, canvassing the state for the constitution, accused the saloonkeepers of trying to sabotage its adoption. Enlisting the aid of Rev. Dinwiddie and other prohibition leaders, he pledged statewide prohibition if they would work for adoption of the constitution and get their followers to bombard Roosevelt with letters for its approval. The strategy worked, and while the official vote canvass required nearly six weeks, it was obvious by September 18 that the constitution had carried.

The official count showed 180,333 for adoption, with 73,059 opposed. Haskell defeated Frantz by a much smaller margin, 134,162 to 106,507, indicating many Republicans had joined Democrats in approving the constitution and statehood. And the separate ordinance for statewide prohibition carried by still smaller margin, 130,361 to 112,258.

On October 25, Frantz took the official canvass report to Washington. Under the Enabling Act, the president was required to act within 20 days. After Frantz' call at the White House, it was reported Roosevelt would issue his proclamation on November 16.

Arrangements proceeded for a gala inaugural ceremony on that Saturday, November 16. Thousands thronged the territorial capital. At 10:15 a. m., Washington time, the president entered the cabinet room—having been delayed several minutes reading his mail—and without ceremony, attached his signature a minute later. As he looked up, Roosevelt exclaimed:

"Oklahoma is now a state."

When the word was flashed to Guthrie, it found Haskell waiting with family and a few friends in room 47 at the Royal. Standing in the center of the room, he placed his hand on the family Bible and quietly took the oath as governor, about 9:30 a. m. Following a symbolic wedding of the territories—Mrs. Leo Bennett of Muskogee, a beauty of Cherokee descent, was the "bride," representing Indian territory, and C. G. Jones of Oklahoma City, the "groom," representing Oklahoma territory—Haskell again was sworn in by Leslie G. Niblack, editor of the *Leader*. For the occasion, Niblack had taken out a commission as notary public—the only official in the switch from the territorial to statehood status eligible to administer official oaths.

To the thousands of spectators, unaware of the earlier ceremony, that moment marked the advent of statehood. They whooped and yelled.

Then as the crowd dispersed to enjoy barbecue in the Guthrie park and to shake hands with the new state officials, "Alfalfa Bill" called the "Con Con" delegates together on the library steps. About two-thirds of the members were on hand as the president declared the convention adjourned sine die. The "Con Con" had come to an end just four days short of a year since the members first met.

CHAPTER III

A Man of Action

"Let us have an administration of worthy deeds, and not of empty words."

AS Governor Haskell closed his inaugural address from the steps of the Carnegie library, the hungry throng jamming the streets gave a burst of applause—and began to disperse, to partake of the big barbecue in the city park. It is doubtful if the full impact of the governor's words registered even with his closest friends, but Haskell already had shown by deeds that Oklahoma had a man of action at the helm.

Oklahoma became a state at 10:16 a. m. eastern standard time when President Roosevelt signed the statehood proclamation. Western Union installed special equipment to flash the news to Guthrie. When the word arrived, Dr. Hugh Scott, secretary to Governor Frantz, rushed into the streets and fired his pistol into the air as a signal to the gathering celebrants. It was about 9:18 a. m. Oklahoma time, and without delay a private ceremony was under way in room 47 at the Royal hotel.

A 1907 campaign button

In the presence of his wife and six children and with only Robert L. Owen, senator-designate, and a few friends present, Haskell stood in the center of the room, placed one hand on the family Bible and took the oath of office. Leslie Niblack officiated.

Then, in anticipation of this moment, Haskell dispatched a telegram to Frank M. Canton in Bartlesville. Canton previously had been selected to serve as adjutant general of the militia. Hearing rumors of an attempt to lay a pipeline across the Oklahoma border from Washington county, Haskell sent Canton to Bartlesville ahead of time to await orders—definite orders from the governor—to stop construction. If industry wanted to use Oklahoma gas, it could locate in Oklahoma; Haskell had determined that this natural resource was not to leave the state.

Canton was the man to get results. He was an uncle of Thomas H. Owen, Muskogee lawyer who had managed Haskell's campaign. While Owen influenced his appointment, Canton was the type to carry out Haskell's orders. He was an early-day peace officer and soldier of fortune who sought adventure in China and Alaska. When under the influence—and Canton was no stranger to the bottle—he might boast of a few notches on his gun. Acting in cooperation with the newly-elected officials of Washington county, he stopped the pipeline crew. The weekly *Enterprise* in Bartlesville reported "this prompt and effective action" is all that prevented the Kansas Gas Co. from connecting its mains to the Oklahoma gas fields.

"Not only was it digging trenches and laying pipe to connect across the line, but it already had a connection made," the newspaper reported. "At two different places, about three miles apart, it had five joints of 16-inch main laid across the line and buried about four feet in the ground. Then to connect the Kansas lines with lines from Oklahoma, all that was necessary was to lay them up to these pipes, fasten them together, and have the thing fixed

"To stop this kind of proceeding, the sheriff's force will tear these pipes out of the ground today, (Nov. 22). They would have done so yesterday, but for the fact that some Kansas teamsters, upon whom they were depending for help, lost their nerve when it came to the pinch, and backed out of the bargain."

Never one to spoil a good show, Haskell kept secret from the multitude his early assumption of official duties and went through the public second ceremony without a flicker. Now that Oklahoma had become a sovereign state, however, the new governor felt free to proclaim the state's independence and, indirectly, to aim a few oratorical shafts at President Roosevelt. Four months before "Teddy" Roosevelt had forced the "Con Con" to yield; now Oklahoma was an independent state, and sovereignty is the key word in Haskell's inaugural address.

"When the sun rose this morning and its brilliant rays spread over our land, it found forty-five sovereign states between the two great oceans," he said. "The sun will set tonight and its last rays will light a grander federation composed of forty-six sovereign states. In its course through the day, the sun will have lighted the pathway of a million and a half of people emerging from the disorder and dis-

FULL PANOPLIED

OKLAHOMA ENTERS UNION

At Exactly 10:16 O'clock President Signs Proclamation.

Governor Haskell and State Officials Formally Inducted Into Office With Ceremonial Pomp and Display of Wild Enthusiasm.

Washington, D. C., Nov. 16--A new star was [illegible] to the American flag today by the admission formally into the Union of the State of Oklahoma. President Roosevelt at ten-sixteen o'clock this morning signed the Proclamation admitting the territories of Oklahoma and Indian Territory jointly as one of the American States

This is the way Leader reported statehood proclamation.

content of bureaucratic government, restricted to the point of helplessness and neglected to the limit of oppression, into condition of liberty and self-government.

"Bureaucratic government, at its best, is impossible of perfection or justice to the people . . . Although Oklahoma becomes one of the federation of states long years after the original compact, it enters that federation with the fullest powers and privileges enjoyed by any of its sisters of riper years. Congress had authority to fix a date when Oklahoma might enter the Union; it had no authority to fix any terms other than those of absolute equality * * *

"Then if we are right that the provisions of the Constitution of the United States shall be respected until changed by the states, we are ready to consider the propriety of the changes threatened by individual construction. Shall the federal government authorize the creation of corporations through its powers and influence; shall interstate railroads be granted federal charters to the extent of depriving the states of home control to the extent that the control now exists? In both particulars, we say emphatically, No! * * *

"An illustration of the inefficiency of federal control of these questions can best be given by calling attention to the practices within the area which is now the state of Oklahoma. Those anxious to centralize this power to control, in the federal government, and advise us to trust our fortunes and our happiness to federal control, must blush when they review the conditions under which we have lived for years. Our freight rates are double those in adjoining states. The lumber trust, the coal trust and other like combinations have fattened by unrestricted robbery of our people.

"If federal control is such a good thing, why is it proven so utterly inefficient in a territory? Let us pray for the reservation within the hands of the people of Oklahoma of the right to govern themselves to the fullest extent that the teachings of Washington and Jefferson contemplated we should have when they created and defended the Constitution of the United States."

Haskell also took note of the recent $29,000,000 fine imposed on Standard Oil—then the anathema of trust busters—by Judge Landis in federal court at Chicago for illegal rebates. The fine, he asserted, "while spectacular to a degree, was more far reaching in its ill effect than the inexperienced author ever imagined.

"As a punishment to the offender, it was nothing. The real of-

NOVEMBER 16, 1907 NUMBER 11

GOV. HASKELL'S

INAUGURAL ADDRESS

Remarkably Keen State Paper by Oklahoma State First Executive

Reviews of Territorial Conditions, Bureaucratic Government, Corporations, Prohibition, Law Enforcement and Policy of the New Administration

Fellow Citizens: You have just been entertained by hearing one of the grandest national airs—The Star Spangled Banner—rendered by a band composed of those whom among all have the first right to the claim of American citizen. There are by [illegible]

proposition, [illegible] The United States stands united against the world, but there are subjects on which some of us differ. There are those who look upon the states as a mere creature of the federal government and subject to the absolute and un- [illegible]

Congress had [illegible] to fix the date when Oklahoma [illegible] enter the union; it had [illegible] fix any terms other [illegible] of absolute equality. [illegible] somewhat at length into [illegible] because of [illegible] certain

A good press agent, Haskell distributed prepared inaugural speech in advance for wide news coverage.

fender might ultimately escape this tremendous money fine. At most, the corporation would ultimately collect the money from the people of the country and laugh at the punishment sought to be imposed. * * * A five-year sentence in the penitentiary would have accomplished more good than a $29,000,000 fine, and the real offender would have paid the penalty, and the public confidence would not have strained in the least."

Then Haskell closed on a happier note:

"We are here not so much for a speech as you are assembled to celebrate this day of Oklahoma's liberty, the day when we can raise the flag of our united country and feel in our hearts the pride of American citizenship, and let us remember now, fellow citizens, that when we gaze upon these beautiful stars and stripes that it has for us in Oklahoma every feeling of pride and sentiment that it has for the people of any other state in the Union, and more. * * * We find the white stripes emblematic of the white race; we find the stripes of red emblematic of the red race, and united beneath the field of azure blue, we join heart and hand, the red man and the white man, in saying Glory! Glory! Long live the state of Oklahoma!

"Let us have an administration of worthy deeds, and not of empty words."

As the crowd moved to the city park, Haskell took his place in the receiving line with other state officials. In frock coat, with bat-wing collar, he greeted the moving line of farmers, tradesmen and politicians passing by. Despite formal attire, he could swap yarns with the best, and every now and then he would single out an individual for personal greeting. Finally, confessing hunger, the governor edged his way to the barbecue pit for a dripping sandwich.

Inaugural visitors found the new governor a handsome man of 47, of stocky build. Standing about 5 feet 10 inches, he weighed around 175 pounds. His friendly eyes were brown, and few gray hairs were visible in his locks of brown.

Only in a pioneer land could a man have climbed the political ladder so rapidly as Haskell. He came to Indian territory in the spring of 1901. Through railroad promotions and the law, he had acquired a fortune in Ohio and New York—sufficient to maintain a private railroad car. Because of Mrs. Haskell's health, he customarily took the family by special car to San Antonio for the winter, and it was on a return trip to the north that the gregarious Haskell met John R. Thomas, a former congressman and one-time federal judge from Illinois, who had settled at Muskogee.

Judge Thomas prevailed on Haskell to stop off in Muskogee and, after private conferences with some of the leading citizens, he was entertained with a public dinner there on April 18, 1901. It was then he advanced plans for building the first of three railroads he would ultimately construct through the pioneer community. It was the Ozark & Southwestern, built from Fayetteville, Ark., through Stilwell and Tahlequah into Muskogee—a project which indirectly would figure later in a spectacular battle involving Haskell, Roosevelt and Bryan.

Haskell established his family at Fayetteville, commuting on weekends from Muskogee, but apparently he considered Muskogee his legal residence from 1901. Four years later, as was noted earlier, he enjoyed such prestige that he could prevail upon the principal chiefs of the Five Civilized Tribes to call the Sequoyah convention to propose separate statehood for Indian territory.

Haskell was born near Leipsic, Putnam county, Ohio, on March 13, 1860. He was the fifth of six children born to George Haskell, a native of Vermont, and Jane Reeves Haskell, a native of Ithaca, N. Y. George Haskell, a cooper by trade, made oak barrels, tubs and other necessities for the farmers of the community. George Haskell died of pneumonia Jan. 9, 1863, leaving Jane to support five children, the youngest a son only nine days old. A daughter had died in infancy.

A resourceful woman, Jane Haskell worked long hours knitting socks, mittens and comforters for her neighbors. She earned $5 a month as janitress in the Methodist church. When Charles was nine he went to live with Thomas J. Miller, a country school teacher, and his wife, Lydia, who had lost at the age of six weeks their only child, a son also named Charles. While Miller attempted to exploit his foster son, working him long hours in the fields and taking his occasional meager earnings from other farmers, Charles was very devoted to Lydia and treated her through the years as a second mother.

Quick to learn in school, Charles by the age of 17 deemed himself qualified to teach country school. With 55 cents advanced by Lydia, he walked 12 miles into Ottawa, the county seat, to take the teachers' examination. He gave the examiner 50 cents. The remaining nickel he spent for a sandwich, then walked home that night.

When Miller failed to locate a school for the boy, Charles called on Squire William Krauss, a German farmer who was president of the

Medarie school board. Squire Krauss promised him a job. Then taking the boy to his cellar, Krauss pointed to seven barrels filled with saurkraut, meat and pickles.

"Your father made every one of those barrels over 15 years ago, and I still use them," the Squire told Charles. "Now if you will teach school as earnestly and industriously as your father made barrels, I shall be satisfied. I am going to give you a trial. You can commence a week from next Monday."

At the close of his second term, Haskell was elected to the Oakdale school which paid him $1.50 a day. Meantime, borrowing law books, he began the study of law and on Dec. 6, 1880, was admitted to the Ohio bar. He continued to teach until March 4 when, approaching his 21st birthday, he closed his school and moved to Ottawa to hang out his shingle as a lawyer.

In Ottawa, Haskell met Lucy Pomeroy, only daughter of Mrs. Justine Pomeroy, widow of a local lawyer. They were married Oct. 11, 1881. Three children were born of the marriage, Lucy dying in March, 1888. In September, 1889, he was married a second time, to Lillian Elizabeth Gallup, a vivacious young woman who was described as a graceful dancer, able horseback rider and a gracious hostess. The second Mrs. Haskell was to follow her husband through the vicissitudes of politics into the national limelight and fortune, his constant companion in campaigns and in public office, his faithful helpmeet in reverses and discouragement.

They also had three children, Frances, Joe and Jane, who would figure to lesser degree in state affairs. Frances and Jane were living to help Oklahoma celebrate 50 years of statehood.

Law led to railroad management and promotion. It was an era of rapid railroad expansion—when railroads were financed on promises, subsidies from transportation-hungry communities and speculation—and expansion led frequently to receiverships and reorganizations, to squeeze out "watered" stock. It was an era when business ethics were about on a par with the morals of an alley tomcat; but Haskell, always resourceful, was able to hold his own—with the best as well as the worst.

In his Memoirs, Murray related a story told by Haskell of a time when a rival railroad blocked an attempted crossing by leaving a string of boxcars on a parallel siding.

"One night I took an engine with some old boxcars in front and started them downgrade, full speed, and knocked the other boxcars off the track," Haskell said. "Then I made my connection in the night time, in advance of any court order."

This experience, incidentally, resulted in a provision in the Oklahoma constitution requiring existing lines to permit an interlocking connection. On June 6, 1887, Haskell incorporated the Finley, Fort Wayne & Western which he desired to build through Ottawa. Denied right-of-way through the town, the young builder assembled ties and rails and recruited extra crews of Irish track layers. Early one Sunday, they worked feverishly to lay the tracks through the town—while the courts were in recess. This experience would find repetition, too, in the removal of the capital from Guthrie in 1910.

In 1896 Haskell obtained control of the Ohio Southern railroad which then extended from Springfield, Ohio, southeast to the Jackson coal field. Within three years, he extended this line north to Detroit and south to Ironton, more than 400 miles. The road later was acquired by Henry Ford and became known as the Detroit, Toledo & Ironton. Other promotions followed in quick order, and eventually Haskell became a familiar figure in New York.

In January, 1900, the chamber of commerce in San Antonio wired him to visit there with a view of building a modern telephone plant. That invitation led to other telephone plant construction projects in Austin, Tyler, Denison, Sherman, Orange, and smaller towns, and with his associates, Haskell also built the first copper toll line from San Antonio to Denison, and set the poles for extending the line from Denison through Muskogee, Vinita and into Neosho, Mo. It was during this period that he met Judge Thomas, and transferred his operations to Muskogee.

In association with William Kenefec of Kansas City and J. S. Keffe of Chicago, who helped raise the capital, Haskell incorporated the Missouri, Kansas and Gulf (now the K. O. & G.) on May 4, 1902, and began construction of a railroad from Baxter Springs, Kan., through Muskogee to Denison. That fall, on October 20, they also began construction of what is now the Midland Valley, from Muskogee through Tulsa, Pawhuska and into Kansas.

Two years later, Haskell also took over construction of the Muskogee street railway system, which he later turned back to the original promoters, but he had the privilege of serving as conductor of the first passenger run, in the summer of 1904. With Morton Rutherford, a prominent Muskogee lawyer, as motorman, he collected fares ranging upward to $5. The run netted about $50 which Haskell gave to the Women's Christian Temperance Union.

Friends used to boast that "Haskell built everything that runs on wheels through Muskogee except the Katy," but he did not confine his activities solely to rails. In 1905, with other Muskogee business men, he purchased a river steamer named the Molly D. He loaded it with cotton and shipped the cargo to the outside world at a neat profit. This successful venture prompted the Muskogee Commercial Club to order a steamboat built to ply the Arkansas. A 125-foot boat of shallow draft, it was named the "City of Muskogee" and operated between Muskogee and Fort Smith.

"Muskogee will become the queen city of the southwest if this navigation is resumed," he remarked. His prophecy thus precedes by nearly 50 years Sen. Robert S. Kerr's prediction of industrial development for Oklahoma through water transportation.

Haskell also organized the Territorial Trust & Banking Co., with a paid-in capital of $150,000, of which he paid half. In 1904, he constructed the first five-story building and hotel, which he named for his friend, C. W. Turner. Then, seeing statehood in the offing, he enjoyed his first spectacular role as vice president of the Sequoyah convention which met in Muskogee Aug. 21, 1905. Haskell was not new to politics, however; an active Democrat, he had supported Bryan for president in 1896. After unsuccessful bids for state senator and for congress, he placed third among seven contenders for the Democratic nomination for governor of Ohio in 1899. When it came to election of delegates to Oklahoma's Constitutional Convention, Haskell saw his opportunity.

Adroitly seeking a dominant role for Muskogee in the Guthrie convention, the business men backed Haskell and Philip B. Hopkins, a Republican banker, on the Greater Muskogee ticket. If the Democrats were in control, Haskell would take the lead; if the Republicans, Hopkins would be the star. When the Democrats scored a landslide, Haskell seized the opportunity to catapult into the governor's chair.

—OKLAHOMA HISTORICAL SOCIETY

Never one to spoil a good party, Haskell is "sworn in" at public ceremony—but he had been governor nearly three hours! Leslie G. Niblack, Leader publisher, obtained notary public commission to administer the oath. Niblack married governor's daughter, Frances, March 31, 1909.

—OKLAHOMA HISTORICAL SOCIETY

A parade in Guthrie business district, enroute to Haskell's inaugural.

Above, **Leslie G. Niblack who administered oath of office; *Right*, Governor Haskell at inaugural barbecue.**

– FRANCES HASKELL COLLECTION

—PHOTO COURTESY FRANCES HASKELL

Miss Jane Haskell (now Mrs. Frank D. Richardson of Miami Beach, Fla.), Mrs. Haskell and, extreme right, Lt. Gov. George Bellamy at inaugural barbecue.

—OKLAHOMA HISTORICAL SOCIETY

Mrs. Leo Bennett, Muskogee, a Cherokee beauty, who was the "bride" representing Indian territory at symbolic wedding of the territories.

—OKLAHOMA HISTORICAL SOCIETY

On way to inaugural, C. N. Haskell rides with Judge Frank Dale and Leslie G. Niblack to inaugural. Mrs. Haskell rode in one of four autos in the parade.

—GEORGE T. HALE PHOTO

Miss Frances Haskell, daughter of the first governor, and Charles N. Haskell II, a grandson, with the Philadelphia flag of 46 stars. The flag is in the Historical society museum.

—OKLAHOMA HISTORICAL SOCIETY

Raising the "Betsy Ross" flag before the temporary capitol in Guthrie June 30, 1908. See Page 76.

CHAPTER IV

The 'Con Con' in Control

THERE was work to be done. While inaugural visitors milled in the park, Governor Haskell returned to his desk. Before the day was over, he had signed appointments to the United States senate for Robert L. Owen and Thomas P. Gore. Then he issued a proclamation calling the first legislature into session for December 2. Anticipating the Herculean task of setting up housekeeping for a new state, the constitution had made special provision for a session of 160 days for the first legislature at $6 a day for the members.

Haskell had some misgivings about the senatorial appointments. The 60th congress was then in session, but when Owen and Gore presented their credentials a few days later, the senate refused to seat them. The senators held that while the governor had authority to fill a vacancy by appointment, that authority did not extend to original appointments from a new state. Owen and Gore would have to await formal election by the legislature.

Oklahomans twittered, meantime, over the double proclamations for Thanksgiving day. Offended by Haskell's personal attacks in the general election campaign, Governor Frantz had refused to ride in the inaugural parade. One of his last official acts on the morning of November 16, however, was to issue a proclamation declaring November 28 Thanksgiving day.

"Oklahoma should be, and is, thankful for statehood, for these material benefits from the Creator's hand, these evidences of substantial worth and worthiness of character in our citizens, and above all for the continued favor the Almighty has shown in these and other innumerable ways," read the Frantz proclamation. Now it was Haskell's turn to ruffle his predecessor. On Monday, he issued his own Thanksgiving proclamation.

"Our people are inspired by a feeling of deep gratitude for the blessings of self government," he asserted, "secured to them by a constitution of their own making with the privilege of self-government under the guidance of Divine Providence, and the honest laborer in all the avocations of life will be given his just reward.

"The patience exhibited by our people during the long struggle for statehood, and the great development of the all but unlimited resources of our state under most adverse conditions, are proof that our people will prosper to the full extent of the opportunity which the new things will afford them, and Oklahoma will enter upon her career of statehood under auspicious circumstances. The financial stringency prevailing not only in the state of Oklahoma, but throughout the Union, is not attributable to any degree whatever to any lack of God's benevolent and abundant blessings, but purely the result of the avariciousness of man. We have, then, to strive for the correction of the practices of men to the end that we may better enjoy the various provisions for the happiness of humanity which the kindness of the great Creator affords us."

In its Statehood edition, the *Leader* reported that of 21 state officials, a decided majority were of southern birth, only five hailing from northern states. All were Democrats. Texas took the lead with five, while Missouri, Arkansas, Georgia and Illinois were in second place with two each.

Of the five new congressmen, James S. Davenport was a native of Alabama; Bird S. McGuire, the lone Republican and former territorial delegate, was a native of Illinois. E. L. Fulton, Oklahoma City, had a brother in the U. S. senate from Oregon. Charles D. Carter, the only native son of the territory embraced in the new state, had been born near Boggy Depot in the Choctaw nation, and came from a prominent family recognized in naming of Carter county. Scott Ferris, the "baby" of the group, was born in Neosho, Mo., in 1878, and settled at Lawton in the Kiowa-Comanche opening of 1901.

When the legislature convened and organized, with Murray as speaker of the house and Johnston as president pro tempore of the senate, Oklahomans discovered that members of the Constitutional Convention dominated all three branches of government. Haskell headed the executive, of course, and three of the five supreme court justices had served in the convention, while a fourth, Jesse J. Dunn of Alva, had headed the Democratic campaign organization to elect delegates to the convention in 1906.

Robert L. Williams of Durant was chosen chief justice. Sam W. Hayes of Chickasha and Matthew J. Kane of Kingfisher were the two other "Con Con" members on the court, with John B. Turner of Vinita as the fifth member. Peculiarly, Pete Hanraty was the only member elected to an executive office, besides Haskell. The former miners' union official was chosen chief mine inspector.

Charles J. West, the new attorney general, celebrated his inaugural by filing a series of 47 suits at McAlester to break the "coal trust." The young Enid lawyer was small of stature and as pugnacious as a bantam rooster. His zeal within months would bring him into conflict with the governor in a feud that reached national proportions, but for the moment, all was harmony in the official family.

West had attained statewide publicity before entering the race for attorney general with a series of rate suits against the railroads. Although a fellow townsman of Frantz, he denied the territorial governor had shown any favoritism in connection with that litigation.

Always a cocksure individual, West eventually became a colonel in the reserves after World War I. One summer at Fort Sill, Colonel West was mounted when boys in the Citizens' Military Training Camp fell in for a field march. From the ranks came an audible whisper, "and a little child shall lead them." West, overhearing the remark, shot a piercing glance at the offender.

"And a little child shall lead them," he repeated, "on a great big horse!" The incident was characteristic of a man bound to clash with the dynamic Haskell.

Even before the inaugural, Guthrie heard disquieting rumors that the new governor might convene the legislature in Shawnee. On November 8, Dr. Hugh Scott, private secretary to Frantz, told newspaper reporters he was the author of a telegram to such effect.

"Currently rumored that the legislature will be called to meet at Shawnee and that all offices will be removed there," he wired Frantz, in Washington. In an interview, West expressed the opinion that the Enabling Act locating the capital in Guthrie until 1913 was not binding since that provision had not been written into the constitution.

Guthrie partisans might have calmed their fears, however, by a careful reading of the constitution. It provided that "the first legislature shall meet at the seat of government" on call of the governor, the date to be not more than 30 days nor less than 15 days after the state's admission into the Union.

Haskell squelched the Shawnee rumor in a written interview with the *Oklahoma State Capital* in which he declared "no thought was ever given to the subject of removal of the capital—so far as I know."

But he added, significantly, "in my judgment, the people can move the capital anywhere in the state they desire, and whenever they desire to do so."

Those who knew "Alfalfa Bill" in later years as a gruff governor could hardly realize how easily he was moved to tears in the early days of statehood. When the delegates gathered around the president's desk in April, 1907, for the first signing of the constitution, Murray choked up and Henry S. Johnston had to conclude his parting remarks. When he was elected speaker without opposition in the Democratic caucus or from the Republicans in the new legislature, Murray was again in tears as he told the house:

"After bearing the ridicule and slander and vituperation of political contest, to receive the unanimous nomination at the hands of my party caucus and to be elected without opposition from the minority . . ." and here Murray broke down, according to the official reporter, Sam A. Oppliger. The house journal shows that Murray's eyes filled with tears; "again and again he strove to master his emotions, and for 30 seconds could not proceed. The immense audience, stilled with listening attitude and contagious weeping for several moments, simultaneously broke forth with tremendous applause" as the speaker resumed "with faltering voice:"

"My friends, after all this . . . this is the happiest moment of my existence!"

Then occurred an unusual tableau. Speaker Murray summoned two elderly men to the rostrum. "One was tall and stooped, the other short and wiry," wrote the *Capital* reporter.

"Gentlemen, you see here the veterans of the Civil war," said Murray, in introducing H. H. Allen and George Dickinson to the house. "One is from the South, and the other is from the North. To prove to you that I make no distinction, I take pleasure in naming these, one a Confederate veteran, and the other a Union soldier, as doorkeepers." The house echoed with applause. Then Murray summoned a somewhat embarrassed Negro to the front.

"The other appointment—that of janitor—I will give to a deserving person. He's a darkie, James Noble. He served the Constitutional Convention well, and stayed 'til the end." Standing "like a statue," Jim Noble took the oath of office; and thus began a career that would make him a familiar statehouse character his remaining years.

Later, Murray had a word of warning for the minority:

"I hope that every member of this legislative body will understand that while I was my party nominee, that I am speaker of every member of this legislative body. I want to say that so long as the Republicans of this body have a desire to promote the interests of this state and desire recognition at the hands of the chair, so long will they have an equal footing on the floor with any member of this body. (Applause).

"But the man who undertakes to get gay, the man who imagines that in a position of this kind, that he can make life miserable for 'Cocklebur Bill' is mistaken . . . If this legislature does the right thing, every member will be praised; but let it do the wrong thing, and every one of you, even those who did right, will be criticized. They will call you one of those fool members of the first legislature. We must go together in the estimation of the people of the state, the good along with the bad . . . Let us go into this work with the determination that the people will be proud always to look back and say the best legislature of Oklahoma was the first legislature!"

Oklahoma as well as the rest of the nation had been in the grip of a money "panic" as statehood approached. On Oct. 28, 1907, Filson, the territorial secretary of state, as acting governor, closed the banks with a proclamation for a six-day holiday through November 2. He declared clearing house associations in the big cities "have entered into agreements to protect themselves against conditions which they apparently are unable to control, and by such action are refusing to ship currency to the country banks which have deposits with them."

From Washington on November 30, Senator-Designate Owen reported that he had assurances that Oklahoma during the next week would receive the $5,000,000 appropriated by congress in lieu of school lands in the Indian territory. He said the funds would be deposited in state banks, thus relieving the financial pinch.

The executive committee of the Oklahoma and Indian Territory Bankers association, meeting in Guthrie on November 25, passed a resolution pointing out that "a stringency exists in the money markets of the United States demanding immediate legislation" by congress. The resolution urged that the "government of the United States become guarantors of all monies due them from banks, and that in lieu of such indemnity by the government that each of such banks shall pay a tax of one-tenth of 1 percent per annum upon the average daily accounts on deposit with such banks." A copy of the resolution was sent to Haskell. Moreover, in his Thanksgiving proclamation, Haskell had taken note of the "financial stringency," which he blamed on "the avariciousness of man."

Thus the stage was set for the governor's message to the legislature in which he launched the new state in the novel experiment of guaranteeing bank deposits. The message read in part:

"The efficiency of government depends upon stability, and in no line of business is stability more important than in banking. Wavering, vacillating, uncertain conditions breed discontent, distrust and ultimate destruction.

"Recent events, in my judgment, make it desirable that the laws of our state should be so reformed as to insure the safety of every dollar deposited in the banks of our state, and to this end, I recommend to your consideration, and hope for the enactment by you, of a code of banking laws upon absolutely safe foundation, and forever relieve the depositors from unrest and doubt, as well as from actual loss."

Haskell further recommended that "the provisions of this section shall apply to all banks organized or existing under the laws of this state, and to national banks which may voluntarily apply in writing to, and be approved by, said banking board for the benefit of their depositors under the provisions of this section."

He also called for enactment by emergency act "of laws providing for separate railroad coaches and waiting rooms for persons of African descent." The governor was keeping his promise to the members of the "Con Con." A guaranty of bank deposits might make national news and set a precedent for the nation, but the governor's declaration for a "Jim Crow" law set off a wave of applause and shouts.

Legislators, anticipating this declaration, already had introduced as bill No 1 in each house "an act to promote the comfort of passengers on railroads, urban, suburban, interurban and street cars" by requiring separate accommodations for white and Negro patrons.

Sen. Clint Graham of Marietta—who had lost to Haskell's maneuvers in the Constitutional Convention—was author of the bill in the senate. Claiming "honors" in the house was Rep. C. A. Skeen of Wapanucka. Sen. Reuben M. Roddie of Ada was credited with authorship of the Depositors' Guaranty Fund bill, although Haskell was consulted and took active part in drafting the measure. Apparently because of the assessment feature, the bill was introduced in the house, on December 5, with Rep. J. Roy Williams of Lawton as sponsor. Tax bills must originate in the house.

As an indication of travel conditions, the audit report of the house disclosed that Rep. Frank L. Casteel of Cimarron county had to travel 462 miles to reach Guthrie—at 10 cents a mile, as allowed by the constitution.

When it came to electing United States senators on December 11 the two houses of the legislature found themselves in dispute as to who should preside in joint session. Senators claimed the distinction for Lt. Gov. George Bellamy of El Reno, while house members contended for Speaker Murray.

"As far as presiding over the body is concerned, I don't care one copper," Murray declared. "What I am fighting for is precedent. This contest is similar to that between the two houses of the national legislature when they are contesting for superiority."

They finally reached a compromise whereby Bellamy would preside and Murray would announce the vote result. With Democrats outnumbering Republicans, 39 to 5 in the senate, and 93 to 16 in the house, there was little doubt as to the outcome. Nevertheless, Republicans placed in nomination Col. Clarence B. Douglas of Muskogee, editor of the *Phoenix*, and C. G. "Grist Mill" Jones of Oklahoma City, civic booster and railroad promoter, who was also a state representative.

Owen and Gore were elected overwhelmingly, although the selection of Gore was in part a tribute to Henry M. Furman of Ada who had placed second in the senatorial primary the preceding June 8. Under a "gentlemen's agreement" proposed by Haskell at the Democratic central committee at Tulsa in March, 1907, it was understood that Oklahoma and Indian territory should each have a United States senator. While senators were then chosen by the legislature, selection was to come from the top candidates.

In the preferential primary, Furman placed second behind Owen, who led the field with 48,885. Furman polled 39,113 to 38,288 for Gore, although the names had been arranged on the ballot to show the candidates from Oklahoma and Indian territories in separate columns. Furman was quoted as saying at the time:

"True it is that the voters gave me second choice for the senatorship, but I am bound by the rule of the committee which, while it cannot bind the people, can bind the candidates. I knew the agreement beforehand, and acquiesced in it. Now both Oklahoma and Indian territories must be represented."

For his gallantry, Furman would be rewarded with appointment as presiding judge of the Criminal Court of Appeals when that tribunal was organized months later. His sacrifice would be recalled also in political conversation years later when, at one time, Lawton had both United States senators, and still later when both senators hailed from Oklahom City. But for the moment, attention focused on Owen and Gore, who were invited to address the joint session. His face beaming, the blind young senator won applause when he observed:

Henry Furman
A "gentlemen's agreement" was a binding contract with him.

"Just 37 years ago yesterday, I discovered America—a little later than Columbus, but it was a greater America. It is befitting that as Oklahoma is the youngest state, I am the youngest senator."

Ten days after the session opened, Haskell prodded the members with a special message: "There are 49 new counties in this state which will be without funds until the first tax collection is made. They are awaiting an opportunity to borrow upon their short-time county bonds and in some instances public schools will close unless relief can be available."

He also advised that the 5-mill ad valorem levy imposed by the territorial legislature in former Oklahoma territory counties "will be delinquent unless legislative action is taken. I still see no just right in collecting a tax from half of the state, when a like levy is not collected from the other half, and unless you find that there is justice in its collection, I would remit the state levy in these counties."

The governor also told the legislature that county attorneys in many counties "advise me of their inability to control what they say is a constantly growing violation of the prohibition law . . . Give us the needed legislation, and we will enforce it. . . ."

Sen. Richard A. Billups of Cordell had introduced a bill providing enforcement machinery for the statewide prohibition ordinance. Promptly dubbed the "Billups booze bill," the measure speedily passed the senate. But it was bogged down in the house by Murray's insistence on a state dispensary system when Haskell, on December 16, appealed to the lawmakers to postpone their Christmas recess "until you have given us ample law to enforce the prohibition provision to the constitution."

"There is scarcely an hour of the day or night but what I hear (particularly from the Indian territory counties) of gross violations of this law—murders, fights and public disturbances. To permit this condition to prevail throughout the holidays will be disastrous to the peace and welfare of the people of the state, and a reflection upon the political party which the people have entrusted to exercise the power of government," he asserted.

Haskell got the recommended tax relief, but the "booze bill" was still weeks from adoption. On January 11, Rep. Henry N. Butler of Pryor Creek injected a little humor into proceedings with this resolution:

"The wind swooped down from the frozen north,
A blizzard swept o'er the prairie;
The legislative cowboys hurried out
To round up Tom and Jerry."

The resolution was referred hilariously to the committee on drains and ditches.

When the legislature reconvened after the recess, Speaker Murray made a ruling which would serve as precedent in counting legislative days for many years—a ruling that during a recess of more than three days, "the pay of both the members of the house and employees thereof shall cease." He also held that the days in recess would not count on the 160 allotted under the constitution for the first session.

When the ruling was reversed in later years, members filed for seven days' pay a week, but counted as legislative days only those in actual session. In modern times, with legislators drawing $15 per day—$105 per week—for 75 legislative days, the pay period usually stretches into the fifth calendar month!

CHAPTER V

Jim Crow and the Guaranty Law

GOVERNOR HASKELL got both the Jim Crow and the Depositors' Guaranty Fund bills, with emergency clause, before the Christmas holidays. The senate version was the bill finally passed for separate coaches. With enforcement in the hands of the corporation commission, railroads were given 60 days to arrange separate accommodations. They also had to display a copy of the law, and so a framed copy of Senate Bill No. 1 became a familiar sight in railroad coaches and depots for years thereafter.

The bank bill, passed December 17, carried a proviso that the deposit guaranty section should become operative 60 days later. Thus, in a matter of 12 days, the first Oklahoma legislature had disposed of the "Negro problem" and had waved a magic wand over the field of economics. It was like repealing the law of gravitation. While some bankers (mostly national) warned that the guaranty law would encourage "wildcat banking" and benefit the imprudent banker at the expense of the prudent, few legislators apparently attempted to peer into the future. In fact, the far-reaching guaranty law took second place in debate and hotel lobby conversation to the discriminatory Jim Crow law.

Perhaps it was just as well. If they had gazed into the future, the shortcomings of the guaranty experiment in the immediate years ahead probably would have caused cold chills; yet, a quarter of a century later Oklahoma's daring venture would serve as the forerunner of the more scientific Federal Deposit Insurance Corp., as we know it today.

Even the hostile *Oklahoma State Capital* hailed its enactment with words of praise:

"The Williams-Roddie bill, an act creating a state banking department and establishing a depositors' guaranty fund, taken up as an emergency bill, is a very needful law and will doubtless do much to allay the financial embarrassment in Oklahoma."

In the same vein, three days later, the *Capital* observed: "The law throughout is a very satisfactory one to both depositors and bankers and will help very materially in bringing about perfect confidence."

The *Guthrie Daily Leader* was more effusive in editorial comment on Dec. 18, 1907:

"Governor Haskell has made history. He arose to the occasion when the people needed action. Without hesitancy, knowing full well that failure meant political ruin, he bridged the awful chasm between prosperity and calamity, tearing loose from all ancient and useless customs. Oklahoma, thanks to a militant chief executive, steps to the fore in the banking world and says, not only to her own, but to all other people, that she will pledge her great, boundless, and widely diversified resources to the protection of their savings. Above the comprehension of the petty partisans, the act will be the star of guidance for ages to come, and proclaimed by the historian as an act of statesmanship undreamed of a year before its adoption as law. Whilst the old regime was wailing and pleading for a wild-cat, elastic currency, begging from the very federal government, Oklahoma, through her native resources, solved a financial problem that was ages old, and no other state will long dare refuse to follow in the procession."

If Editor Niblack assumed the state was guaranteeing deposits, he was revealing a careless reading of the bill. Yet it was an easy error to make and within months some banks would be advertising for deposits with just such a claim. Their action brought a sharp warning from the bank commissioner and the second legislature went farther, to make it a misdemeanor to so advertise. Banks might advertise that deposits were covered by the guaranty fund, but they must not imply that the resources of the state were back of the guaranty.

But Oklahoma had a panacea for panics and bank failures! Why hadn't some one thought of such a plan before? As a point of historical accuracy, the idea of bank guarantees was nearly a century old—although the Oklahoma plan appears to have been an outgrowth of the more immediate Populist movement in the depression-ridden '90s.

In an exhaustive study of the bank deposit guaranty movement in 1920, Thomas Bruce Robb, then associate professor of economics at the University of Missouri, traced the history from the Safety-Fund banking system inaugurated in New York in 1829. It provided for a special fund to guarantee all debts of the banks. The intention of the law was to provide security for note issues. Bank deposits were so little developed at the time that apparently the New York legislature overlooked the fact that bank debts might also be occasioned by deposits. The panic of 1837 caused widespread bank failures, and the debts of failed banks were such that the safety-fund system broke under the strain.

During Populist days, there was continuous agitation for bank deposit guaranties, and a serious attempt was made during one session of the Kansas legislature to enact such a system. Following a report from a Populist bank commissioner on Sept. 1, 1898, recommending such a law, Governor Leedey, also a Populist, called a special session of the legislature to enact such a law. The bill passed the senate and lacked only four votes in the house.

In 1908, despite opposition from William Howard Taft, the leading contender for the Republican nomination for president, and other national G. O. P. leaders, Gov. Edward W. Hoch of Kansas advocated such a program following national publicity on the Oklahoma plan. Kansas, along with Nebraska, South Dakota and Texas, did follow Oklahoma's lead in 1909, but with guaranty systems on a somewhat different basis.

Warning signs were ignored as Haskell and his bank commissioner, H. H. Smock, prepared to put the Oklahoma plan into operation on Feb. 15, 1908. As Eugene P. Gum, veteran secretary of the Oklahoma Bankers association, would point out in 1941 in a resume of banking history, "there was a hodge-podge of banking practices in territorial days." When settlers first poured into Oklahoma territory, there were no banking laws. The banks established in the new country were private banks, not subject to examination or supervision by either territorial or federal authorities.

On Feb. 18, 1901, President McKinley signed a bill granting the corporation law of Arkansas to the Indian territory, but all supervision was federal. Banks could incorporate under this act, but were not compelled to do so, and charter banks were not given further statutory regulations.

In Oklahoma territory, the situation was different. The year after the opening, the territory was organized with its own legislature, executive officers were appointed from Washington, and the corporation law was taken from the Nebraska code. In 1897, a banking law was passed which required all banks to incorporate and place themselves under supervision of a bank commissioner. Four different commissioners served between 1900 and 1902. Funds were inadequate for supervision, and commissioners were further harassed because banks were allowed to move without giving notice.

If a bank was not prospering in one town, the officers would move to a more promising location. One commissioner's report showed seven banks not examined for the year because the examiners could not find them! Later they were prevented from moving by a legislative enactment. A bank could incorporate with a capital of $2,500, and even a third of that could be invested in real estate and fixtures.

As originally passed, the new bank law made no requirements for capital structure. But twice before the legislature ended its session in May, changes were made in the law, one amendment outlining minimum capital investment. For cities of less than 2,500, the minimum was $10,000; for 2,500 to 5,000, a minimum of $15,000; for those in the 5,000 to 10,000 bracket, $20,000, and for cities of more than 10,000, a minimum of $25,000. Also, a director had to have at least $500 invested in bank stock.

When Haskell signed the bill in December, Smock advised the banks:

"All provisions of this bill are now in force except the guaranty of deposits, and that provision will become effective Feb. 15, 1908. Only clean and well-managed banks, conducted in harmony with the law and in condition to pass rigid examination, will have the benefit of the Depositors' Guaranty Fund."

To assist Smock in checking the condition of the banks, Haskell—in typical Haskell fashion—picked up the telephone and appointed 31 bankers to help in examinations. After they had made 515 examinations in January and February, the banks were allowed to continue operations even though some could not comply with requirements. Smock explained this laxity in his first annual report:

"On account of the unfavorable financial situation at this time, it was extremely difficult in many instances to meet every requirement immediately. If the bank was solvent and showed a disposition to comply with the law as promptly as possible, the department endeavored to be fair and give them an opportunity . . . While a large number of banks were technically not in harmony with every provision of the banking laws, their general condition was such that the department did not feel justified in closing them and upon their promise to correct the objectionable features of their business, they were allowed to continue in operation."

The law followed closely the outline given in Haskell's message to the legislature. He had called for creation of an advisory board, to be known as the state banking board. The governor, lieutenant governor and president of the state board of agriculture were made ex-officio members. Then he recommended that the board be authorized to levy an assessment "upon each and every bank subject to the provisions of the banking laws of this state, equivalent to 1 percent of the deposits of such bank."

The assessment was to be collected by the bank commissioner in such instalments and at such times as the board might direct. The amount so collected was "to constitute a reserve fund, to be known as the Depositors' Guaranty Fund, for the protection of bank depositors in each of said banks as may thereafter become insolvent." It was proposed that the guaranty fund should be maintained at a figure equal to 1 percent of the average daily deposits.

"Many big state bankers were opposed to the law," Gum reported, in a post mortem before the Colorado Bankers association in 1924, "but assumed a passive attitude because of the popularity of the movement at the time, relying on their belief that the law could be declared unconstitutional." The court attack was not long coming.

The banking board issued a series of monthly postcard summary reports which reflected a flow of deposits to the guaranty-fund banks. In a card on June 27, 1908, the board declared:

"Bank reports show that the effect of the law began weeks before the law was in actual operation. There are now 551 banks under the law in this state, including 54 national banks. There are 255 unsecured (i.e., national banks not under the fund) in the state . . . From Dec. 3, 1907, to Feb. 14, 1908, the deposits in the unsecured banks decreased about an even half million. The secured national banks for the same period gained in deposits about $520,000. State banks (all secured) for the period from Dec. 11, 1907, to Feb. 29, 1908, show an increase in deposits of $716,749.47."

The postcard report then traced other increases since the plan went into operation. By May 14, deposits were up $645,413 in secured national banks, $2,344,602 in state banks, while unsecured banks showed a decline of $600,807. The report cited a total increase between December and June of $4,237,765, while deposits in the unsecured banks dropped $1,100,807. "After deducting $691,453 for a decrease in state fund deposits," the report boasted:

"So it is apparent that there is $3,828,410 more individual deposits in banks in Oklahoma than before the Depositors' Guaranty Fund was passed, and the secured banks have been the beneficiaries."

The banking board, authorizing an initial assessment of 1 percent for the year 1908, called for the first instalment of one-half of 1 percent on February 17. Almost immediately the constitutionality of the law was challenged by the Noble State bank. Losing in the district court, the Noble bank appealed to the state supreme court where the appeal was pending when the guaranty section had its first test.

On May 21, Smock called Haskell from Coalgate to advise that he had discovered "gross irregularities" in the conduct of the International bank of Coalgate. That was at 2:15 p. m. The governor authorized the commissioner to close the bank, and immediately he called a meeting of the banking board. Within 42 minutes the board had taken this action:

"It is moved by C. N. Haskell, seconded by J. P. Connors, that the bank commissioner now present at Coalgate be directed to proceed immediately to pay off any approved depositors requesting payment of deposits to them, drawing on the cash on hand, all available in other banks, and for any deficiency upon the treasurer of this board."

It was a presidential election year, with the Democratic national convention called for Denver in early July. In Oklahoma, the first legislature was nearing the end of its long session, and the bank closing rated only secondary mention in state papers. But in the nation, the swift operation of the depositors' guaranty fund was a matter of widespread interest.

The Coalgate bank had deposits of about $38,000. Smock reported about $9,000 in cash on hand, with $7,000 available through deposits in other banks. J. A. "Sunny Jim" Menefee, the state treasurer who also was treasurer of the board, left that night for Coalgate to assist in paying depositors.

Within three days, most of the depositors had been paid. In fact, the story spread of a telephone call to a depositor living in the country. When it was explained that he could get his money, the farmer was quoted as saying, "well, I'm in no hurry. I'll be in next week."

Whether true or not, the story was good enough to repeat at Denver where Haskell told it before a group of admirers as evidence of the efficacy of the guaranty plan. But there was another side of the story from the bank officials. That was an open charge by Dr. L. A. Conner, the bank's president, that the bank was closed "for no other purpose than to make a demonstration of the depositors' guaranty law for the Democratic convention at Denver." That charge would come later, however, when Haskell had his hands full with other troubles.

Two incidents in February, 1908, reflect the spirit of the robust era. The first, involving J. A. Tillotson, a member of the house from Nowata, centered around the frantic efforts of oil promoters to get a lease on the 110-acre allotment of Frank Tanner, a Delaware Indian. The land was in the heart of a "hot" oil play in Nowata county.

Harry F. Sinclair, once a traveling salesman, had struck it lucky in the oil business and was then operating from Independence, Kan. Sinclair got a promise from the young Indian to sign the lease on his 21st birthday.

But a few days before that event, Tillotson had Tanner in Guthrie. Tillotson was working with C. J. Wrightsman, a Tulsa oil man. Seeking to escape Sinclair, the young Indian was hurried to Oklahoma City, and later, by automobile, to Enid. Sinclair kept the long distance operators busy until he learned Wrightsman and Tanner had checked in at an Enid hotel about 10 p. m., two hours before the Indian would become of age.

Unable to get even a freight train to Enid, Sinclair chartered a special train at Guthrie, the *Oklahoman* reported, and taking Tillotson along, dashed through the night for his date with Tanner. There at an Enid hotel, the oil men worked out an agreement whereby Tanner received $20,000 for a short-term lease.

"Tanner is an intelligent Indian," the *Oklahoman* added. "He hugely enjoyed the experience."

Sinclair was reported as saying, "It was a good fight. The compromise is satisfactory." Four years later, Sinclair, then a multi-millionaire, would launch Haskell in the oil business. And as the result of a much "faster" oil deal, he would touch off the Teapot Dome scandal which resulted in prison for one member of the president's cabinet, disgrace for another and jail for the oil man. Wrightsman, likewise blessed with the migic touch in the oil business, became immensely wealthy; but when he tried his hand at politics, with races for the U.S. senate in 1924 and 1930, he discovered that money alone will not win elections.

The other incident which produced arched eyebrows in some circles and chuckles around the legislature occurred at Norman. Two university co-eds, pledges of Phi Delta Gamma, were given assignments to shave a corpse in the anatomical laboratory at the University.

—OKLAHOMA HISTORICAL SOCIETY

Signing the "Billups Booze bill' March 24, 1908. The ceremony was moved to the senate chamber because the light in the governor's office was too dim for pictures. Sen. R. A. Billups, Cordell, is in left foreground, Mrs. Billups back of him; Mrs. Haskell, as usual, is at her husband's elbow, and Rep. William Murdoch, Ralston, chairman of the house prohibition enforcement committee, is at her left. Dry leaders and legislators make up the remaining group.

THE PHILADELPHIA RECORD, SUNDAY, JULY 5, 1908.

LEADING FIGURES IN FOURTH OF JULY CEREMONIES AT INDEPENDENCE HALL

Mayor W. H. Hornaday, of Guthrie

Beech Newell reading the Declaration

MURPHY FOR GUFFEY

MOLLIES KILL THEIR MAN

Continued From First

A contemporary account of "Betsy Ross" flag ceremony in Philadelphia July 4, 1908. W. H. Hornaday was from Lawton, Col. T. H. Soward from Guthrie. See Page 76.

William H. Murray III, with "sight unseen" constitution which his grandfather carried in metal box. Secretary of State is charged with "sacredly" preserving this parchment document.

—GEORGE T. HALE PHOTO

—OKLAHOMA HISTORICAL SOCIETY

"Alfalfa Bill" Murray dictates to secretary, Sam A. Oppliger, on farm near Tishomingo.

—OKLAHOMA HISTORICAL SOCIETY

'he Murray family at farm home. There were wo future governors in this group.

—OKLAHOMA HISTORICAL SOCIETY

Elected the day after 37th birthday, blind Tom P. Gore served 20 years in the U. S. senate.

Governor Haskell and Secretary of State Bill Cross in governor's office at Lee-Huckins hotel June 12, 1910. Photo from Oklahoma Historical Society.

Miss Florence O. Wilson, niece of W. F. Harn, lent this photo of Mr. Harn on site of future capitol. He donated 7½ acres from farm staked in "run" of 1889 for statehouse structure.

Above, Guthrie still bemoans "stolen seal." *At right,* Earl F. Keys with Great Seal taken from temporary capitol night of June 11, 1910; Bill Cross in background. A George T. Hale photo.

While a group of medical students kept guard at the doors, the young women gave the cadaver a close shave.

"No, I wasn't afraid," one of the girls told a reporter. "It wasn't half as bad as shaving a real live man would be."

What made the event doubly interesting in political circles was that one of the girls was Winn Ledbetter, daughter of the "Con Con" member. The other was Inez McMillian of Pauls Valley.

Reaction to the Jim Crow law was sporadic. Republicans opposed

The Oklahoman *for Feb. 18, 1908, carried this pointed reminder that Jim Crow law was in effect. Roy E. Stafford, Democratic state senator, was then editor.*

the measure in the legislature, but when E. P. McCabe, a Negro who had served as assistant auditor in the territorial government, attacked the law in federal court, his suit was thrown out on a technicality.

John Golobie of the *Oklahoma State Register* was one of the few newspapermen to editorialize against the law. Pointing out that the special census of 1907 showed only 112,160 Negroes in a total population of 1,414,177, Golobie wrote that "the percent of Negro population in Oklahoma does not warrant Jim Crow legislation . . . The extreme Jim Crowists are like the foreign anarchists, who bring over a righteous hatred of their own government and transplant it against our own. They absorb their prejudices in localities in the South where there were 10 Negroes to one white man, and are trying to apply it here in Oklahoma where there are 12 white men to one Negro."

When Democrats in the legislature chartered a special train to Muskogee for the state convention on February 22, the train was peppered with rocks at Red Bird, a Negro community in Muskogee county. Jack Love, the hefty chairman of the corporation commission, dispersed the Negroes with a fusilade of pistol shots.

CHAPTER VI

County Seats and 2-cent Fares

SO many cities were eager to challenge the county seat selections of the Constitutional Convention that the first legislature finally laid down the rules for county seat elections in a bill offered by Sen. J. Elmer Thomas of Lawton. It provided that an election might be called by the governor on petition signed by 25 percent of the voters, and the county seat could be removed on majority vote except in instances in which the original county seat was within six miles of the geographical center of the county.

In such cases, the law required a 60 percent vote for removal, unless the contesting city was at least one mile nearer the geographical center. Then the majority rule applied. No county could expend funds for a courthouse or permanent improvements before April 1, 1909, unless it had first voted on a county seat location. Once a county seat was established under this procedure, there could not be another such election within 10 years.

Haskell approved the Thomas bill in April, 1908, and the county seat fights were on. Within months, 30 county seat elections were held and two new counties—Harmon and Swanson—were created.

These county seat battles provoked tense feelings, but most elections were orderly under supervision of out-of-county supervisors designated by the governor. After Eufaula lost to Checotah on May 23, 1908, however, a delegation of Checotah citizens invaded the town on Sunday, June 7, and one man was killed. As the *Indian Journal* reported the melee, the Eufaula residents were taken by surprise. Coming from church, they found armed members of the Checotah delegation deployed in the business district.

The *Journal* told of one Checotah man taking a strategic position "with Winchester at his hip, ready for action. His first orders were given to Deputy Constable (F. M.) Woods and Deputy City Marshal (Harry) Keiser to get off the streets and out of town else he would give them the contents of his gun.

"This warlike declaration . . . was a signal to the rest of the invaders to clean their deck, ready for action . . . As soon as the astonished citizenship of Eufaula realized what an ungodly act was to be perpetrated on so holy a day, men with stern and grim-set faces began to emerge with such protecting arms as could be gotten on short notice and immediately the battle lines were formed."

During a temporary truce, Woods attempted to disarm one of the Checotah men and was fatally wounded. Meantime, Ed Julian, the county clerk and a Checotah partisan, had opened three offices in the courthouse and others were dumping records into large sacks. Following the shooting, cooler heads prevailed, and the Checotah crowd withdrew. On the Monday following, Julian shot and killed an elderly man at the Foley hotel, but when he was removed to the jail at Muskogee, he sent word the shooting had nothing to do with the county seat fight.

Although the vote had been 1,647 for Checotah, 1,200 for Eufaula and 384 for Stidham on May 23—a clear majority for Checotah—the supreme court held months later that mutilated ballots should have been counted in ascertaining the total vote. On that basis, Checotah was 27 votes short of a majority and Haskell ordered a new election on Feb. 10, 1909. That time, Eufaula won, 1,919 to 1,843. The *Journal* promptly invited Checotah folk "to come to the county seat . . . the question is forever settled; erase the past and begin life anew."

Sayre retained the county seat of Beckham, defeating Erick by 11 votes, 1,883 to 1,872. But at least eight county seats named by the Constitutional Convention lost to rivals. Among them were Westville, in Adair, to Stilwell; Kenton, in Cimarron, to Boise City; Lehigh, in Coal, to Coalgate; Grove, in Delaware, to Jay; Pond Creek, in Grant, to Medford; Ryan, in Jefferson, to Waurika; Tecumseh, in Pottawatomie, to Shawnee, while Grand, in Ellis county, not only lost to Arnett, but faded from the map. It had been the county seat of old Day county, which was abolished by the convention.

Harmon, carved out of parts of Jackson and Greer counties, was formed May 22, 1909, by vote of 1,418 to 323 within the area involved. It was named for Judson Harmon, former U. S. attorney and later governor of Ohio, in recognition for his assistance to the early settlers. When the U. S. supreme court, in tracing the true channel of Red river, had detached the 1,500,000 acres of old Greer county from Texas in 1896, Harmon had espoused a plan whereby homesteaders could buy an additional quarter section on liberal terms.

Swanson, named for Gov. Claud Swanson of Virginia, was created out of parts of Comanche and Kiowa counties in May, 1910, but promptly ran a gauntlet of litigation which ended with its dissolution by the state supreme court in 1911. With Mountain Park and Snyder contending for county seat honors, Gov. Haskell selected the former by lot in issuing his proclamation to recognize the county on Aug. 13, 1910.

Some time later, all the Swanson county officials but the sheriff decided to move their offices to Snyder, contending that Mountain Park had failed to live up to its promises to provide suitable quarters. Following the 1910 general election, Sheriff W. E. Brashears sent deputies out in January to round up the county commissioners and take them to Mountain Park to approve his bond. A farm hand was killed when the deputies sought forcibly to take C. E. Bull, chairman of the board, to the official county seat.

The vote to create the county had been 1,918 to 907 in the portion of Kiowa county sought to be detached, with Snyder (population 1,200) casting 795 ballots. In the Comanche county area, however, the vote was 323 opposed to 80 for the new county, and since this portion lacked the 60 percent required under the law, the supreme court held the election invalid. Swanson county officials were forced to surrender their records under threat of district court contempt proceedings.

James V. McClintic, an affable traveling salesman who had come up from Texas to settle in Snyder, was elected to the third legislature from Swanson in 1910. He later went to congress for several terms.

While the first legislature was still grinding away, the newly organized Corporation Commission was bringing the railroads and utility corporations to terms. In compliance with the 2-cent fare provision of the constitution, two principal railroads announced fare reductions at statehood. E. P. Ripley, president of the Santa Fe, wrote Henry Asp, the railroad's attorney in Guthrie, that the Santa Fe would put the new fare into effect November 17. B. F. Winchell, president of the Rock Island, announced similar plans during a visit in Guthrie.

One of the first acts of the new commission was to direct railroads to establish state line stations. Thus a traveler into or through the state could take advantage of the 2-cent fare at that point.

The commission consisted of Jack Love, the Woodward cattle man, and two Confederate veterans, J. J. McAlester of McAlester and A. P. "Potato" Watson of Shawnee, so nicknamed because of his success as a potato grower. A 248-pounder who stood nearly 6 feet 6 inches tall, the colorful Jack Love was a striking figure at the inaugural, towering over other visitors and surrounded by a bevy of teen-age girls he had brought from Woodward for the occasion.

Love escorted the girls home over the week-end, then returned to be elected chairman of the commission. He was a natural for the job. A native of Texas, where his father fought in the War of Independence under Sam Houston, Love was an intimate friend of Temple Houston, Sam's son, who had enlivened many a trial in the frontier settlement with his picturesque and unconventional courtroom manners.

A man of action, like Haskell, Love had his personal feud with the railroads. From many trips to market with cattle, Love had experienced the hardship of travel in crowded cabooses and from the "public be damned" attitude of the railroads.

The story spread around Guthrie some weeks later that Love had received a call from the president of the Santa Fe. Since the only chairs in his office were occupied, a clerk brought a chair for the caller, but Love waved him back.

"Let the president of the Santa Fe stand—he's kept the people standing long enough!" Love barked. Whether true or not, the story reflected the chairman's attitude.

The commission operated on an individualistic basis. There were three members, but for all intents and purposes, Love was the commission, and he stood ready to assure "fair dealings" between the corporations and the public, individually or collectively.

Promulgated order No. 1 required the railroads and express companies to file copies of each tariff schedule to enable the commission "to have every bill referred to it checked, and advise the parties whether or not they have been overcharged." In the first annual report, the commission claimed this action resulted "in saving thousands of dollars."

Murray relates in his Memoirs an instance in which a Tishomingo merchant received some freight and showed Murray the bill, asking if the charge weren't excessive.

"I told him I didn't know, but the commission had the rates and I advised him to write a letter, sending his receipt for the freight. As soon as Jack Love got this freight receipt, he called the rate clerk and said, 'Get the rate on this.' Finding the railroad had charged $2.50 excess, Jack Love turned to the stenographer and dictated a letter that in substance read:

"'George W. Dudley, a hardware merchant at Tishomingo, was charged so much for so many pounds of freight from St. Louis to Tishomingo. That is an excess over and above the rate of $2.50. You will, therefore, immediately send me a draft of $2.50, payable to George W. Dudley.' The railroad did so. In one year, they collected more than $7,000 in those early days for shippers of small amounts of less than $10. It came to be known as the most serviceable wing of the government."

Order No. 4 required railroads to open the ticket windows an hour before train time, and to clean up their depots. After hearings in which the roads submitted evidence that they would operate at a loss on the 2-cent fare prescribed in the constitution, the commission granted exemptions to the Fort Smith & Western and four other small lines.

The commission ordered depots built in 33 towns during its first year, including Seminole and Woodward. When the commission received a petition for day-time train service between Marietta and Guthrie, in August, 1908, it directed the Santa Fe to institute such service with a train leaving Marietta at 5:30 a. m. and arriving in Guthrie at 11:20. Return trip was specified to leave Guthrie at 5 p. m.

The order was typical of the personal interest taken by the commission.

"It appears to the commission this would be a great convenience to the country merchants who buy goods at Oklahoma City, and to parents who have children attending the university at Norman," read the order. "They could visit that institution all day and return the same day; and the further fact, that there are many people who have business at the capital of the state, which could be transacted in half a day."

During the year, the commission received 308 complaints, including 271 against railroads, 17 against telephone companies and eight against telegraph companies. Some 125 were adjusted without hearing, but the report showed evidence taken and orders issued in 77 cases.

When Love learned the commission secretary, W. L. Chapman, was receiving outside compensation from the railroads for furnishing statistical information to the railroads, he promptly ordered Chapman's dismissal in the face of political pressure. The commission had a firm policy, Love declared, against employees taking extra pay from any corporation.

When Love was up for re-election in 1912, he was unopposed for the Democratic nomination and won easily in the general election. His colleague, "Potato" Watson, was destined to become the first official impeached and removed from office—when a later legislature caught the commissioner accepting "free" gifts of coal!

Less than three months after the corpse-shaving incident, the University faculty was under investigation by a special committee of the board of regents, consisting of Cruce, Rev. N. L. Linebaugh of McAlester and C. J. Pratt of Oklahoma City. *The Oklahoman* on May 14 reported a "house cleaning" imminent.

"Card playing, dancing, cigarette smoking and other allegedly immoral practices are charged against the professors in a letter written to a member of the board by the Rev. R. E. L. Morgan, pastor of the M. E. Church, South, at Norman," the paper asserted. A group of faculty members retained J. B. Dudley as attorney and threatened suit unless Morgan retracted his charges.

Faculty members were called "one by one" into executive session in the office of President David R. Boyd and "given to understand that dancing, card playing and other practices detrimental to the moral advancement of youth should be discontinued." In turn, faculty members left the junior-senior reception later "as soon as dancing began, but the dancing continued without interruption."

Dr. Boyd, at the University since 1892 as its first president, was not considered for reappointment and the board dropped six other faculty members at its meeting June 23, 1908. Dr. A. Grant Evans was elected president by unanimous vote.

"Politics is all that removed me," Dr. Boyd told a reporter. "I do not know the other men, but those relieved of their positions are thorough, scholarly and capable, and do not deserve to be peremptorily dismissed because of outrageous charges—charges that were entirely false and . . . nothing short of damnable."

Dr. Boyd declined an honorary degree of LL.D. the following June, but on March 31, 1930, was elected president emeritus in recognition of his services to the state.

CHAPTER VII

Nine-Foot Sheets and 'Old Sunnybrook'

THE first legislature completed its 160 days on May 26, 1908. Faced with the Herculean task of setting up "housekeeping" for a new state, the lawmakers had run the gamut from a bill to eradicate Johnson grass to the "Billups booze bill." Indirectly, its acts had added "Old Sunnybrook" to the lexicon of political jargon and the fun poked at the requirement for nine-foot sheets in hotels probably minimized a full appreciation of the more praiseworthy achievements.

Jim Crow and the Depositors' Guaranty Fund bills passed early, but in May the legislature wrote an entirely new banking law fixing, among other provisions, minimum capital investment requirements. Other statutes provided for staffing the state departments, creating the Criminal Court of Appeals, and appropriating $50,000 to move state convicts from the Kansas penitentiary in Lansing to McAlester and start construction of the state prison there.

Among new revenue measures was an income tax, levied on a graduated scale on incomes of $3,500 and more, and a gross production tax. Since the immediate problem was for financing a state government without ready revenues, the legislature authorized a $1,400,000 funding bond series. Officials were forbidden to employ blood relatives or in-laws under an anti-nepotism law, while another measure directed railroads, pipeline companies or other corporations taking land under eminent domain to pay immediately into court the appraised value.

"Our law makes the matter speedy, simple and with a minimum amount of court expense, and gives the land owner his pay more promptly than three-fourths of the other states in the Union," Haskell observed, in a summary of the legislature's accomplishments. "Thanks to Senator Thomas." The Lawton senator, who also had fathered the county seat bill, was destined to advance eventually from a distinguished career in the legislature to a record 24-year tenure in the United States senate.

Other laws required railroads to equip their locomotives with electric headlights of 1,500 candlepower and to maintain repair shops in the state for equipment used in Oklahoma. In approving the bill by Speaker Murray requiring the teaching of agriculture in the public schools, Haskell noted that Murray had sponsored similar laws in both the Sequoyah and state constitutional conventions. He sent the speaker the pen used in signing the bill on May 20, 1908.

Another bill by Murray and Rep. George C. Whitehurst of Beckham county provoked chuckles in the nation's press. It was the so-called "nine-foot sheet" bill—a measure requiring hotels and sleeping car companies to equip their beds with sheets long enough to fold back three feet over the top coverings. It also called for knotted ropes in guest rooms in hotels of two stories, and iron fire escapes in taller buildings.

"They made a heap of fun out of this measure," Haskell said in his review, "but both of these were very necessary and proper provisions of the law. Any traveling man can tell you that the nine-foot sheet is the best sanitary measure possible in a state like ours, where 50,000 strangers, sick with consumption, traveling back and forth from the north to the south, occupy the sleeping cars and hotels, and breathe into the heavy blankets and comforters. You can't tell when the blanket or comforter was last washed, but you can easily tell whether the sheet is clean, and fresh, and a nine-foot sheet gives you a sufficient length to fold back over the edge of the blanket and protect yourself from any disease that might have been in the bed or berth the night before."

The Johnson grass bill made it mandatory on county commissioners, once advised of a growth of the wiry grass along a roadside, to direct the road overseer to see that it was eradicated.

The "Billups booze bill"—named for Senator Richard A. Billups of Cordell, the author—provided enforcement machinery for the prohibition ordinance. The bill passed the senate early in the session, but Haskell's plea for a law by Christmas to check the liquor traffic failed to budge the house. Speaker Murray was insisting on a state dispensary system which would make beer, wine and whisky available for medicinal purposes on a doctor's prescription.

Murray had to wage a vigorous fight for the amendment in the house, arguing that the purpose "is to allow law-abiding citizens legally to obtain intoxicating liquors when needed without violating the law."

"When law-abiding men are not put to the necessity of violating the law," he maintained, "they will aid in the enforcement of the law.

Otherwise, law-abiding citizens, compelled to violate the law, will not assist in its enforcement." He also argued that "liquor is not fit for a beverage, but is a medicine, particularly in ailments of 'flu, pneumonia and other pulmonary distempers."

When the bill returned to the senate, the senators flatly rejected Murray's plan. But when it became obvious the speaker would not yield, the senate in mid-March finally accepted the amendment and the dispensary system went into operation. Haskell appointed R. L. Lozier of Blackwell as state agent. Lozier contracted for "Sunnybrook" as the state's official brand, and "old Sunnybrook" became a term to provoke knowing smiles in political circles for years thereafter. The posted retail price—on doctor's prescription—was 80 cents a pint, $1.60 a quart or $5.40 a gallon. Of course, a doctor would have to recognize an imminent epidemic to prescribe a gallon!

The senate won one concession, however, in accepting the dispensary plan. It provided for submitting the question to the voters in the first referendum on November 3. When the measure failed, 105,392 yes to 121,573 no, Haskell promptly abolished the dispensary setup—only to revive dispensaries in some 20 cities upon petition of the citizens, under the provisions of the original prohibition ordinance adopted with the constitution.

Apparently mindful of the county boundary fight in the early days of the "Con Con," Haskell discouraged the legislature from establishing new state institutions. One bill passed, however, to create an Industrial Institute and College for Girls—without appropriation or location—and another for four secondary schools of agriculture. This bill empowered a special board to locate these junior colleges. The board included J. P. Connors, president of the board of agriculture; E. D. Cameron, state superintendent of public instruction, and Dr. J. H. Connell, president of the Oklahoma A. and M. college.

One school located at Tishomingo was named for Speaker Murray; another was located at Goodwell, and took its name from the panhandle. Three guesses as to where the Cameron school, at Lawton, and the Connors school, at Warner, got their names!

Connell's election to the presidency of Oklahoma A. and M. college in January, incidentally, had been the forerunner of more extensive changes in the faculty at the University of Oklahoma. Dr. Connell, then living in Dallas, replaced Dr. A. C. Scott, a Republican. For 10 years director of the experiment station at Texas A. and M. college, Dr. Connell was editor of the Texas Farm and Ranch magazine and president of the Texas Farmers' congress when elected to the Stillwater post.

Doctor Connell's qualifications kept criticism of the change at a minimum, but when the board of education removed Dr. David R. Boyd, the first president of the university, and dismissed a number of faculty members, there were widespread charges of political domination. Dr. Boyd was succeeded by Dr. A. Grant Evans of Tulsa, a former Muskogee resident and friend of Governor Haskell. Dr. Evans had played an active role in the Sequoyah convention.

The *Outlook,* edited by Dr. Lyman Abbott, finally took up the charges of political interference and the changes drew national attention. Meantime, the legal question of whether the board of education or the university's board of regents had jurisdiction was settled in favor of the regents, and that board ratified the changes. Haskell had appointed his primary opponent of 1907, Lee Cruce, as chairman of the board of regents, and Cruce defended the action as without political significance.

But the man in the White House was taking note of developments in Oklahoma and the *Outlook* charges would furnish another round in President Roosevelt's arsenal when he trained his guns on Haskell in the spectacular battle of the year.

Incidentally, the appointment of Cruce to the board of regents was typical of Haskell's efforts to convert former enemies. The year before, he had asserted, among other vicious charges, that four of the Ardmore banker's campaign managers were ex-convicts. He included in that category Moman Pruiett, the famous criminal lawyer, who had gone to prison in territorial days. Cruce men returned the compliment with photostatic copies of old judgments against Haskell, charging the Muskogee man was a "dead beat." But never one to carry grudges, Haskell selected Paul Nesbitt, a Cruce lieutenant, for a position in his office and sought to mollify Cruce with the regents appointment.

Meantime, the legislature approved the location of the Western Oklahoma Hospital for Insane at Fort Supply, where the territorial government had been permitted to take over a former military reservation.

On May 19, the *Oklahoma City Times* related the pathetic story of the removal of 400 patients from the Norman hospital. It was an era in which the mentally ill were regarded as lunatics and potentially dangerous. The sheriffs of Cleveland and Woodward counties, with

12 deputies each, were on hand to supervise the loading.

The patients, many in tears, were herded on a special train. The loading was completed about 5:30 p. m., and the dispatch added: "The train will run without stop to Tangier, a small flag station about nine miles from the hospital, and the patients will be transferred to wagons and vehicles." Dr. E. G. Newell, of Yale, a member of the Constitutional Convention, was appointed hospital superintendent at Fort Supply. The removal left about 300 at Norman, but Indian territory patients returned from Missouri soon boosted the total again.

When the legislature passed an appropriation bill to meet unpaid bills of the Constitutional Convention, Haskell vetoed an item of $298 for mileage and per diem for himself.

"I believe no body of men ever worked more unselfishly or with more patriotic feeling than the delegates in the Constitutional Convention," he wrote. "I personally know that many of them continued at their posts of duty, laboring for the welfare of the people of the state, when they were living on their own means and reduced to the point where they had to practice the greatest economy, to be able to pay their expenses out of their own pockets."

In explaining the item veto, Haskell said he felt "I have no right in the exercise of my present official authority to use that official power to approve and secure payment of my own claim . . . It has been my judgment from the beginning that this, like other convention bills, is a just obligation of the United States government . . . Even should the legislature see fit to overrule this veto, I should still decline to accept the money from any source other than the United States government."

Murray had presented bills totaling $80,153.28, including $45,349.13 for clerical hire and $31,991 for mileage and per diem for the delegates. As president of the convention, he advised the legislature that he had expended more than $3,000 from his own funds. The money had been borrowed from Tishomingo banks and it was not until he was ready to leave for his first trip to South America in 1919 that he finally got the loans paid off.

The house promptly overrode Haskell's veto of the $298 item, but there was no provision made for reimbursing Murray for the $3,000. In a will executed in 1919, Murray made bitter reference to this old debt and the 10 percent interest paid over the years. In the will, now published for the first time, he asserted:

"This is an obligation of the State of Oklahoma, but which the politicians in control of the several legislatures since the first have steadfastly refused to pay. In the first legislature . . . I did not make claim for this sum, although reporting it as used for the state, out of a sense of propriety because of my control of the first house of representatives. I then thought I could rely upon future legislatures to recognize the justness of the claim as well as provision for the correction of the record of the Constitutional Convention, which duty was placed upon me by the said convention . . . If there ever come a time that the politicians of the state of Oklahoma shall have reformed their minds and consciences to such extent that they can get away from their own selfish, petty ambitions sufficiently to recognize this claim, which has proven a burden upon me, it is then my will that they pay this claim . . . to my wife or heirs; but it is also my will that neither my wife nor my heirs shall ever ask the politicians or the state to recognize this obligation of the state's."

As Murray approached his 80th birthday on Nov. 21, 1949, a former statehouse reporter (the author) organized Squirrel Rifle Brigade No. 2 to honor "Alfalfa Bill" and to square this old debt. From 14 states and two foreign countries came contributions which eventually totaled $2,700.

Then almost blind, his familiar muffler wrapped around his throat, Murray told a crowd gathered on the fourth floor of the capitol:

"I appreciate deeply this manifestation of respect. I was a little bit astonished to find I am to have a monument before I died (it was dedicated in May, 1950, at Tishomingo). Few men have received such honor. I know but one—the great American, Benjamin Franklin."

Murray told then why he had carried the "sight unseen" constitution with him in 1907. He said he caught a copyist making changes in the article on corporations, and dismissed him.

"I never trusted anyone, and I didn't file the original even though seven lawyers in the convention advised me to," he added. "The people in Milburn, near my home, met and condemned me for not filing the original copy of the constitution with the secretary of state. I knew what I was doing, and nothing in hell could change me."

With the legislature out of the way, Haskell could turn his attention to the coming national convention. An original supporter of Bryan in 1896, he had basked in the limelight during the "Great Commoner's" visits in June and September, 1907, and again in December, when Bryan spoke to the legislators. Bryan, on the other hand, had not only declared the Oklahoma constitution "the best ever written," he had looked upon the Depositors' Guaranty Fund law as a foster child. In fact, he had indorsed the principle in an interview in January, 1908.

"Lack of public confidence is what drives money out of circulation," he said. "Restore public confidence, and money returns to its accustomed channels. For lack of confidence, the best remedy is insurance of bank deposits, and I have urged upon the various states and congress the passage of some measure similar to the law adopted by Oklahoma." The interview was widely circulated.

While weighing the bills left by the legislature, Haskell was faced with the decision of permitting the state's first execution. James Ford, a Negro farmer convicted of killing his wife, awaited the gallows at Frederick in June. When the governor refused clemency, Sheriff Frank Carter proceeded with arrangements for the hanging. He built a scaffold back of the jail, inclosing it with a plank board fence. There were plenty of cracks, however, and the execution drew a crowd of knothole watchers including boys who would be recounting the event 50 years later.

Frank Carter
The first official hanging led to long state career.

Sheriff Carter, defeated for state auditor in his first bid in 1914, was elected in 1918 and continued in state office for nearly 30 years. In his more mellow moments, he too would recall the story of the first hanging for wide-eyed young reporters. Thus the hapless Ford was immortalized in recurring feature stories, while the venerable Carter went on winning elections.

When the legislature adjourned, Murray went on the $2 a day pay schedule provided in the constitution for legislators after the then $6 daily salary period ended. After compiling the House Journal and winding up the session's business, he found he needed $90 to pay debts and get back to Tishomingo. He went to Joe McNeal, a Republican banker, for a loan. Then as Murray relates the incident in his Memoirs:

"He replied: 'You are one honest presiding officer. I will let you have it.' He made out a note for $93, and I may state here that Judge Will Chappell knows of this transaction. He was attorney for the bank and a member of the house; and I want to observe also that his conduct in the house was as good as any Democratic member, although a Republican.

"I replied to Mr. McNeal: 'What do you know about honest presiding officers?' He answered, 'This bank has been the clearing house during the territorial times.' Then I asked, 'do you know any member of the Constitutional Convention that was bribed?' He answered, 'not one.'

" 'Any in this house?' 'Only six in your house. Now,' he said, 'Murray, I could not swear positively, but my experience as a banker handling money, my observation and experience in such things in the past that were duplicated, I know that there were bribes.'

"Then he added: 'You know Mr. So-and-So, he was known as the oil lobbyist. Every one knows that. There is a little fellow around here, rather mouthy, that only the wise know what he is doing. He is the go-between to ascertain what member can be bribed.

" 'Some two or three weeks ago six large envelopes were brought into this bank. They were fluffy, full of paper, and I could swear according to my judgment, they were filled with money bills. There was written across each of them these words: "This package is filed in escrow to be delivered to (naming the person—all six of the names were separately on the six packages)" when this little go-between said so. * * *'

"He said finally this little fellow came in and said, 'Deliver all six of those packages.' He wanted to know what it was for, and he looked up the legislative journal and found it was the date following the vote on the gross production tax on oil; that all of those fellows had voted against the bill."

On the afternoon of June 30, Haskell participated in a colorful ceremony when the "Betsy Ross" flag with 46 stars was raised on the Masonic flagstaff in front of the temporary capitol. The first regimental band of the Oklahoma national guard turned out in full regalia, and Company D was in formation as the old flag of 45 stars came down and the new colors were flown to the breeze.

It was a proud moment for the ladies of the Betsy Ross association who had gathered at the Carnegie library a fortnight before to sew the stars and stripes together for this new flag. Ninety-two women prominent in the state were selected to make the stars—one for each side—and the flag measured 12 by 20 feet in size.

Among those at the sewing bee were Mrs. Haskell, Mrs. Charles H. Filson, Mrs. Henry E. Asp, Mrs. Bird S. McGuire, Mrs. J. H. Burford, Mrs. H. S. Cunningham, of Guthrie; Mrs. William J. Pettee, of Oklahoma City; Mrs. Patrick S. Nagle of Kingfisher; Mrs. Leo Bennett (the "bride" representing Indian territory in the inaugural "wedding"), Mrs. C. W. Turner, Mrs. Clarence B. Douglas and Mrs. Thomas H. Owen, Muskogee; Mrs. Don P. Wills, Chelsea; Mrs. Ben LaFollette, Checotah, and Miss Kate Barnard, the commissioner of charities and corrections.

After the ladies had completed the flag, they were entertained at a banquet in the Ione hotel, where the flag was prominently displayed on the dining room wall. Then they formed the Betsy Ross association, with Mrs. J. J. Brotherton of Muskogee as president. The association motto was "patriotism," and the members vowed to hold annual meetings.

Now, as the flag waved in the afternoon breeze, Haskell paid tribute to their work.

"As American citizens, we are assembled to view and admire the first flag of our country bearing the 'Star of Oklahoma,'" he told the assembled throng. "Just as the wedding ring is the symbol by which you unite the heads of the family, so are our stars and stripes the symbol under which we Americans have united to make one grand and glorious country * * *

"The ladies of our state have responded to the call of the community and have made this flag. They have woven upon it the firm pledge to the freedom and loyalty of Oklahoma. Their names will go down in history by virtue of their helping make this flag."

When the flag was lowered, it was delivered to a delegation comprising members and sons of the Grand Army of the Republic which departed the next morning for Philadelphia for the first national display of the forty-sixth star. Under an act of congress passed in 1818, when a new state joins the Union, the flag bearing the latest star is unfurled officially over army posts and government stations on the July fourth next.

Thus, Philadelphia had arranged a celebration at Independence Hall honoring Oklahoma.

In the delegation, proudly carrying Oklahoma's "Betsy Ross flag" were Col. T. H. Soward of Guthrie, W. H. Hornaday of Lawton, R. M.

Conder of Bristow, T. G. Elder of Newkirk, Judge Hosea Townsend of Ardmore and William Querry of Tulsa. In exchange for the Oklahoma flag, the delegation received as a gift from Philadelphia another flag made in the home of Betsy Ross, the seamstress credited with making the first stars and stripes banner in Revolutionary War days.

Through telegraphic communication, simultaneous celebrations were arranged for Philadelphia and Oklahoma.

"With the first stroke of noon from the big clock in the historic tower, the Oklahoma flag was unfurled to the skies, and a salute was fired by a battalion from the Sixth regiment," the *Philadelphia Record* reported. "To add to the impressiveness of the occasion, the sun burst through the bank of clouds, which during the two hours the exercises had lasted had every minute threatened a downpour, and at the very

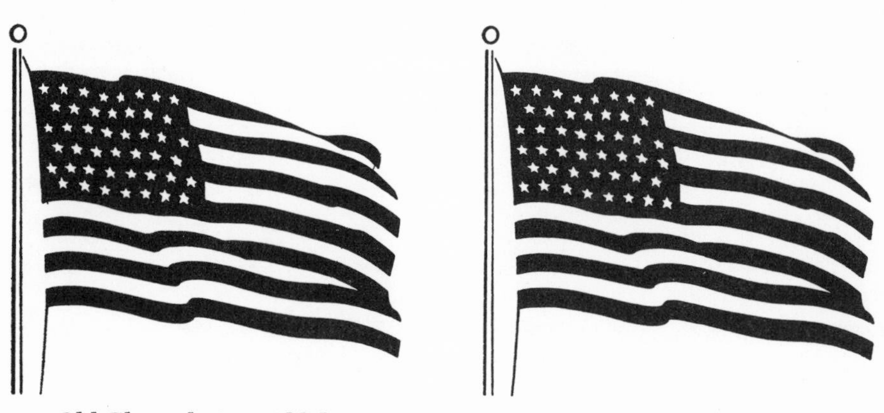

Old Glory—before Oklahoma. *New flag of 46 stars.*

It was necessary for War Department to re-design the flag when Oklahoma became a state. New flag was unfurled officially July 4, 1908.

instant the folds of the banner caught the light breeze, the bright rays lit up the flag, bringing out its colors in strong relief against the dark background. At this good omen a shout went up from the crowd, but was quickly hushed to permit several hundred children from the Matthew Baldwin school to lead in the singing of the Star Spangled Banner."

At that moment, Mayor John E. Reyburn sent this message to Oklahoma:

"Philadelphia sends greetings to Oklahoma. The flag is raised. The people here have sung the 'Star Spangled Banner.' "

And back came the reply from Acting Governor Bellamy:

"Thanks for your recognition. Oklahoma returns greeting of Philadelphia. Our people have just sung the 'Star Spangled Banner,' 'Red, White and Blue,' and 'America.' "

Colonel Soward, the delegation chairman, launched into a eulogy of Philadelphia, for honoring Oklahoma, and lauded the youngest state.

"You may think me an optimist, but I am willing to be called that," he told the assemblage. "This nation is now the greatest in many respects, and Oklahoma will in the future play no small part in its greatness."

On July 2, the *Oklahoma State Capital* reported that Oklahoma's "big four"—Haskell, Murray, Chief Justice Williams and J. B. Thompson of Pauls Valley, the Democratic state chairman—had left the night before for Lincoln, Neb., to confer with Bryan and national leaders of the Democratic party. The youngest state was edging into the limelight on the eve of the national convention.

CHAPTER VIII

The Haskell-Roosevelt Fight

FROM Lincoln, Oklahoma's "big four" went to Denver where Governor Haskell was chosen chairman of the resolutions committee. Denver, "the city of lights," beamed with hospitality. Each new delegation was met by a band and escorted to its hotel along streets banked at choice locations with snowdrifts. The snow had been hauled from the mountains, and the more adventurous delegates were invited to enjoy the novelty of a snowball fight in July.

It was a foregone conclusion that Bryan would win the presidential nomination on the first ballot, but it took about 60 hours—with frequent telephone conferences with the "Great Commoner" in Lincoln—to shape the platform. Many of the resolutions were drafted to woo the labor vote, but Haskell was perhaps proudest of the plank on banking. It read:

"The panic of 1907, coming without any legitimate excuse, when the Republican party had for a decade been in complete control of the federal government, furnished additional proof that it is either unwilling or incompetent to protect the interests of the general public. It has so linked the country to Wall street that the sins of the speculators are visited upon the whole people * * *

"We pledge ourselves to legislation under which the national banks shall be required to establish a guaranty fund, prompt payment of the depositors of any insolvent bank, under a suitable system which shall be available to all state banking institutions wishing to use it."

Neither mountain snow nor public acclaim could soothe the governor's mounting irritation over the news from Oklahoma. Three days after Haskell left Guthrie, Attorney General West had slapped an injunction suit against the Prairie Oil & Gas Co., a Standard Oil subsidiary. As a foreign (i.e. out-of-state) corporation, the Prairie company did not enjoy the right of eminent domain in acquiring pipeline right-of-way as did Oklahoma companies. On this ground, West obtained from District Judge A. H. Huston a temporary order halting further work on a pipeline from Caney, Kan., into the "shallow sand" oil district of Washington and Nowata counties. The action was closely parallel to Haskell's own course on the day of the inaugural, but now the governor took an opposite attitude. Haskell wired Lieut. Gov. George Bellamy to halt the suit.

The *Capital* depicts Bryan's telephone conferences with delegates in Denver.

"If he finds the law being violated, he should report facts to governor for his consideration," the telegram added. "I am satisfied he is misinformed, but of course I may be mistaken, that the attorney general should report to governor's office and await instructions. I will not tolerate any other procedure. Please let me hear fully."

When the telegram was forwarded to West, the attorney general promptly wrote the governor "your request comes too late to stop the filing of the suit, nor can I now dismiss the suit already filed * * * It would be so simple for the Prairie to domesticate and so useful to the people of the state that I cannot understand why we do not all demand this thing unitedly, instead of part of us seeking to bind the other part as to law and the facts.

"When Owen (the operator halted by Haskell on inaugural day) operated without authority, it was seemed to be unlawful. Big and little look alike to me, as far as I am concerned; my policy can be nothing but enforcement of all the laws."

Smarting from such defiance, Haskell upon his return promptly sought a writ of prohibition from the supreme court against the attorney general, and the high court held with the governor. Shortly afterwards, Haskell was honored with selection as treasurer of the Democratic national committee. National recognition was slight balm, however, for the troubles ahead. In the controversy with West, his name had been linked with Standard Oil, and to be identified with this odious "trust" was political poison. In a matter of days, the flareup set off a chain reaction which brought the governor into open conflict with President Roosevelt in a welter of charges with national repercussions.

On Aug. 17, 1908, Omer K. Benedict, editor of the staunchly Republican *Oklahoma City Times,* was arrested for criminal libel on complaint of the governor. The arrest focused attention on a short editorial in the *Times* for August 14 commenting on Haskell's challenge to meet William Busbee, Dennis Flynn and Bird McGuire at 16 picnics in the state "and discuss matters face to face."

"He says Busbee controls the *McAlester News,* and Bird McGuire the *State Capital,* and Dennis Flynn the *Times,* and for that reason he wants to meet them face to face," the *Times* added. But the stinger was in the next paragraph:

"He says he is holding office, and people have a right to know what he is doing. That's true, governor. What were you doing in the Coats house, Kansas City, Mo., on the 16th of June in company with Mr. O'Neil of the Standard Oil Co.? And what were you doing in Independence, Kan., on the 17th with Mr. O'Neil when you were supposed to be in Muskogee? And please tell us, who were you supposed to meet in Chicago? If you correctly answer the first time, we'll compliment your honesty. If you evade the question, the *Times* will tell who you were going to meet, and what for."

Jim O'Neil of the Prairie was in disfavor with Oklahoma oil men, largely because of the glut on the market from the prolific Glenn pool near Sapulpa. Because of limited pipeline connections, oil was stored in surface ponds, or permitted to flow down streams, and the price fell to as low as 25 or 30 cents a barrel.

Shortly after Benedict's arraignment at Guthrie, William Randolph Hearst entered the fray. Although the New York publisher had supported Bryan in 1896 and in 1900, he was vigorously opposing the Democratic nominee in person and through his nine newspapers in 1908. Under the guise of backing the Independence Party, Hearst on September 12 displayed an affidavit from Frank S. Monnett, former attorney general of Ohio, based on an incident in 1899. Monnett charged he had been approached by one C. B. Squires with an offer of a $400,000 bribe to halt prosecution of Standard Oil. He quoted Squires as saying his associates were Frank Rockefeller and C. N. Haskell.

The charge was not exactly news. It had been contained first in Monnett's official report of 1896-99, a copy of which was filed with the Ohio supreme court. And it had been the basis for an incident which enlivened the closing days of the 1907 campaign when the Republicans imported John M. Sheets, Monnett's successor as attorney general of Ohio, to speak in support of Frank Frantz' candidacy in Oklahoma City and Guthrie.

Waving a copy of Monnett's report before his cheering partisan audience, Sheets centered on Haskell's name and added:

"According to Monnett, the other two men are Frank Rockefeller of Cleveland, O., brother of John D., and Charles B. Squires, formerly of Cleveland, now of New York City."

Furthermore, Sheets asserted, $500,000 was to be spent by Standard Oil in an effort to quash the Ohio prosecutions, and of this sum, $100,000 was to go to Haskell and Squires for their services as "go betweens." It had even been arranged, he said, to put Monnett's $400,000 in a lockbox at a bank to await his retirement from office. Although an investigation by the court failed to connect Standard Oil with the bribery offer, the fact that Monnett was approached and offered such a bribe "remains undisputed in part of the records of the supreme court of Ohio," Sheets declared.

Democrats, somehow anticipating this last-minute Republican attack, brought Monnett to Oklahoma to speak for Haskell. Described as a "Roosevelt Republican" with independent views, Monnett came from Columbus, O., to speak Sept. 12 in the same convention hall where Sheets had leveled his charge. Monnett first took up the matter of judgments—the Republicans had spread photocopies of numerous judgments in New York and Ohio naming Haskell as defendant—and asserted:

". . . I notice in the evening paper (*Times*), and it has been appearing for three or four days, they say that Haskell was sued. I think there is a lot of suits they have not got in yet. I want to go one better; Charlie Haskell was doing about $30,000 a month business; paying it out in labor, in ties and iron, and doubtless he had debts and was sued, and I think I know Ohio attorneys too well. They would not let a man go all these years without some of it . . . If Haskell has put as many railroads through, and if he has robbed as many of these Wall Street plutocrats as these Republican papers say, he has been going some."

Now the partisan Democrats stomped and yelled with delight.

"They say out there with us that a born drunkard is the worse kind of man to make war against saloons, and if he (Haskell) is as bad a man as they say he is, he is up to all the tricks of these corporations, and he would be a good man to have in the governor's chair, a good man to carry out the provisions of the constitution. What are the facts?

"Charlie Haskell has stood in my judicial district, first as a young lawyer; and as a contractor, he went up against such men as Calvin Brice and Sam Thomas, and he asked no odds or quarter from any of them. He was a veritable young lion, and they knew it. And the only surprise is that he is out here in politics.

"Haskell never was a politician; he always would say what he thought. I think if you search his record through, you will learn that Charlie Haskell defends every bit of it . . . From the very first moment the charge was made, Haskell stood ready to straighten it out. He was ready to come and testify, but Sheets told you, and the records show you, the case was dismissed before he had a chance to testify. C. N. Haskell stood ready to testify from the moment the charge was made, and this was made on the answer of Squires.

"When they asked him whom he represented, he said, 'Frank Rockefeller and Haskell.' We named those as he gave them, and the name of Haskell appeared—Haskell of Cleveland, O. Now, there is another Haskell in Cleveland—I don't remember his initials, but his name was Haskell, and he lived in Cleveland, and he was often in the city. He was connected with the (Mark) Hanna and Rockefeller crowd, and it was very easy to confuse the two. Charlie Haskell was not living in Ohio at that time. He was living in New York, and the moment he heard the charge, he offered to come back and testify—was anxious for an opportunity to come back and face the charge, and Charlie Haskell was the only one in the bunch who ever was.

"Squires fled the state. This other man Haskell has never been in the city since, and I say to you that if Haskell were guilty, it was the sworn duty of Sheets, as attorney general, to bring him back and convict him. . . . Do you suppose C. N. Haskell, the man who would stand for 112 days and fight all comers to put these provisions against trusts in this constitution—do you suppose he is as likely to be the man mentioned as that other Haskell, employed by the corporations, who has fled the state ever since?"

Eager for statehood, and already surfeited with the acrimonious ballyhoo of the campaign, the Oklahoma voters apparently took little heed of this remarkable exchange between Sheets and Monnett. Nor did Hearst's revival of the Monnett charges on Sept. 12, 1908, provoke immediate fireworks. His principal target was Senator J. B. Foraker, the Ohio Republican whom Taft had disavowed in the midst of the campaign for his link with Standard Oil. But when the publisher repeated the charges, naming Foraker and Haskell as the tools of Standard Oil in a speech at St. Louis a week later, Roosevelt took note.

"Apparently Mr. Haskell got out of his work for Standard Oil the chairmanship of the platform committee of the Democratic national convention," shouted Hearst. "In the front rank of Democracy stands C. N. Haskell, along with those other patriots and martyrs—Roger Sullivan, Tom Taggart, Murphy and Pat Moran"—(all Democratic bosses).

Roosevelt was itching to get into the fight, as his correspondence with Taft, published years later, would reveal. On September 21, he wrote Taft:

"Why don't you in your speech point out the fact that Haskell, whom Hearst has shown to be the tool and agent of the Standard Oil Co., is now the treasurer of the Democratic national committee, and as soon as he was selected Chairman (Norman E.) Mack announced that the Democratic campaign chest contained $300,000 that was left over from the last campaign? Either this makes perfect nonsense of Parker's reiterated statements that they did not get much money in the last campaign or, what is more probable, it shows that Mr. Haskell's appointment means Standard Oil money for Mr. Bryan. Bring this out, and smash and cut Bryan about it."

Alton B. Parker had been the Democratic nominee against Roosevelt in 1904.

Publicity-wise, "Teddy" Roosevelt long ago had learned to capitalize on the week-end news lull for a "better play" for his pronouncements from the White House. Now he fired a week-end blast at Haskell. Bryan promptly rushed to the defense of Oklahoma's governor with a lengthy telegram to the president.

"In endorsing this charge," he wired, "you attacked the Democratic party and its candidate, saying that 'Governor Haskell stands high in the councils of Mr. Bryan, and is the treasurer of his national campaign committee.' And you add that the 'publication of this correspondence not merely justified in striking fashion the action of the administration, but also casts a curious sidelight on the attacks made upon the administration, both in the Denver convention which nominated Mr. Bryan and in the course of Mr. Bryan's campaign.'

"Your charge is so serious that I cannot allow it to go unnoticed. Governor Haskell has denied that he was ever employed by the Standard Oil Co. in any capacity, or was ever connected in any way with it or with the transaction on which your charge is based.

"Governor Haskell demanded an investigation at the time the charge was made, offering to appear and testify, and he demands an investigation now. I agree with you that if Governor Haskell is guilty, as charged, he is unfit to be connected with the Democratic national committee and I am sure you will agree with me that if he is innocent, he deserves to be exonerated from so damning an accusation.

"As the selection of Governor Haskell as chairman of the committee on resolutions at Denver and treasurer of the national committee has my approval and endorsement, I feel it my duty to demand an immediate investigation of the charge against him endorsed by the president of the United States. Your high position, as well as your sense of justice, would prevent your giving sanction and circulation to such a charge without proof and I respectfully request, therefore, that you furnish any proof which you have in your possession or, if you have no proof, I request that you indicate a method by which the truth may be ascertained."

In a stinging reply, Roosevelt declared Haskell "unworthy of any position in our public life." Before making his reply, however, he called to the White House one W. C. Haskell of Cleveland who, it developed, was then superintendent of weights and measures in Washington. That Haskell denied he was the one involved in Monnett's charges. Roosevelt's letter, drafted after a long session with the cabinet, was published nation-wide. Wrote Roosevelt:

"In your telegram you speak of so much of the charge against Governor Haskell as dealt with his relations, while in Ohio, with the Standard Oil Co. You omit the charge as to his relations with the Standard Oil interests, as shown by his action as governor of Oklahoma, this very summer, this action being in part taken while he was at Denver, where, as you state, he was by your wish made chairman of the committee which drafted the platform upon which you are standing. In my statement, I purposely made no specific allusion to the Ohio matter, and shall at this time make none, in spite of its significance, and in spite of the further fact that Governor Haskell's close relations with the Standard Oil interests while he was in Ohio was a matter of common notoriety.

"In Oklahoma, it is a matter of court record. By this court record, it appears that the attorney general of the state, elected by the people, obtained an injunction to prevent the Prairie Oil & Gas Co. from building a pipeline; and that Governor Haskell found this out while he was at Denver, as appears by the representations for dissolution of the injunction made in his name on behalf of the state before a court of superior jurisdiction to that which issued the injunction.

"In this the governor states that the acting governor, in his absence, had asked that the hearing be postponed until he, the governor, might return and have an opportunity to investigate the controversy. The governor sets forth in his petition that he is the sole authority to determine such matters, and that the attorney general and the judge in the lower court had no right in the case and that the action of the judge of the lower court represented 'an encroachment by the judiciary.'

"The attorney general opposed the dissolution of the injunction, stating that the Prairie Oil & Gas Co. was a foreign corporation which had not accepted the provisions of the constitution applicable to such corporations, and that without authority of the law it is employing a great force of men and teams to dig up, across and into various highways of the state for the purpose of laying its pipelines. The governor prevailed, the injunction was suspended, and the pipeline was permitted to continue its work, to use the words of the attorney general, 'without any color of law.' "

After tracing in detail the corporate ownership of the Prairie, to establish it as a $10,000,000 subsidiary of Standard, Roosevelt continued:

"Let me add that Governor Haskell's utter unfitness for any public position of trust, or for association with any man anxious to make an appeal on a moral issue to the American people, has been abundantly shown wholly irrespective of this action of his in connection with the Standard Oil interests. As an American citizen who prizes his Americanism and his citizenship far above any question of partisanship, I regard it as a scandal and a disgrace that Governor Haskell should be connected with the management of any national campaign. . . .

"You close your telegram by saying that you expect and will demand fair and honorable treatment from those who are in charge of the Republican campaign. I am not in charge of the campaign, but greatly interested in it. I have shown you above, fairly and honorably, that Governor Haskell is a man who, on every count I have named, is unworthy of any position in our public life. No further investigation of these facts is required. They are spread on the record before you, and they were available before Mr. Haskell was chosen for his position of treasurer."

After reading Bryan's telegram in the press, Dennis Flynn, campaigning for United States senator, wired his friend Roosevelt:

"Just read Bryan's letter to you. You are perfectly safe in submitting the entire matter to the Democratic attorney general of this state."

From Haskell's standpoint, Attorney General West didn't help matters. He gave an interview approving the president's "mild rebuke" of the governor.

In a statement to the Associated Press, Haskell termed the Prairie Oil & Gas Co. charges "a joke on Mr. Roosevelt's stupidity," adding that he had done nothing that would confer on the Standard Oil subsidiary any more authority than it already possessed under a franchise granted by the Interior department.

But the onslaught from the White House was too devastating, and Haskell hurried off to Chicago where, after conferences with other members of the Democratic campaign committee, he sent his resignation to Chairman Mack. The latter was in New York. Usually Haskell's letters were well framed, grammatically, but the resignation letter discloses his agitation in the poor structure of the opening sentence. It read:

"Since the president and his cabinet have joined forces with Mr. Hearst and three Wall Street brokers to make a personal fight against me, notwithstanding the president in his answer to Mr. Bryan abandoned his charge about the Standard Oil cases, if by all means at the command of the government and the millions of Hearst and his Wall Street allies, they persist in vicious, unwarranted and untruthful attacks on me personally, I welcome the call and shall meet it with all the vigor at my command. I shall treat them all as private citizens and subject to the penalties of the law which they merit.

"In this I know I shall have the aid of my neighbors at home for proper purposes; but my time must be free from other demands here. Again my heart is full of hope for the election of Mr. Bryan and

(John W.) Kern. Honest government and rule by the people is at stake . . . I would not for one moment consider remaining in any way connected with the committee. Therefore, I tender my resignation as treasurer of the Democratic national committee that not the slightest contest of my own could in any way be used by the president to cloud the sky and shield our opponents from discussing the real issues and laying bare the Republican duplicity to the people."

A delegation of about 100, including some members of the militia, state officials and employees, and a band welcomed Haskell back to Guthrie. His wife, first to meet him, was weeping as they embraced. The *Capital* reported that the governor took up the four charges against him "and attempted to explain his innocence. He started in on Dennis Flynn, whom he characterized as the king grafter of Oklahoma; he said Bird McGuire was a disgrace to the state, and that President Roosevelt is a damnable scoundrel and infamous liar.

"He said he would show up these three gentlemen to the world, and that the personal life of all of them would be flashlighted to the public gaze. He said that his resignation was not asked for, but that he resigned for the reason that if Bryan should be defeated, he did not want it said afterward that 'Had Haskell resigned, Bryan would have been elected.'"

Bryan eased out of the controversy with a letter to Roosevelt on September 26. He declared that since Haskell voluntarily had resigned, "I need not discuss the question of his guilt or innocence, further than to say that the public service which he has rendered and the vote of confidence which he has received from the people of his state ought to protect him from condemnation until the charges can be examined in some court where partisanship does not bias and where campaign exigencies do not compel prejudgment . . .

"I have never been informed of any charge that had been made against Mr. Haskell connecting him with Standard Oil or any other trust. I had known him as a leader in the Constitutional Convention of Oklahoma, and had known him as one of the men principally responsible for the excellent constitution which has since been adopted. . . . I had known of his election to the governorship of that great young state by a majority of 30,000; and I had known that the constitution was adopted and Governor Haskell elected in spite of the efforts of your administration and in spite of the speeches made in Oklahoma by Mr. Taft."

Haskell celebrated his return by filing suit against the State Printing Co., Dennis T. Flynn, Bird McGuire and John H. Burford for $195,062.18 representing money received by the printing firm from the territory of Oklahoma from 1891 to 1907, inclusive, plus interest.

Frank Greer, the *Capital's* militant editor, displayed an account of the suit under a two-column headline: "More Free Advertising," and asked facetiously why the governor hadn't made the suit for an even $200,000; that would have been more impressive! The editor denied the three other defendants owned, or had ever owned, any interest in the company.

At Omaha on October 16, a deputy sheriff broke down the door of a stateroom to serve Hearst with papers in a $600,000 slander and libel suit. The petition on Haskell's behalf was filed hurriedly that day when it became known the publisher would be passing through Omaha on a Union Pacific train.

Meantime, the governor launched a campaign for public subscriptions to carry on his fight. He said he had not sought the appointment as treasurer, but had accepted "because Oklahoma, through the united effort of its whole people, had obtained the high standing that made the national committee willing to honor our state . . . I believe that thousands of Republicans in Oklahoma felt that I was doing my best, unselfishly and impartially, to aid in advancing the standing of our state; but, unfortunately, within our own borders there is a political band of grafters, selfish interests and oppressive monopolists that have no pride in their home city, nor their home state, unless it yields to them advantages and profit.

"Not a drop of red blood flows through their veins—not a spark of patriotism warms their heart for Oklahoma. This crowd immediately began the most damnable effort to destroy and villify me that any man has ever been subjected to." Then he fired another salvo at Roosevelt:

"You have clearly demonstrated by hearsay judgment and vacillating from one charge to another, by admitting that various charges were without foundation, therefore abandoned, and yet without displaying the manhood to apologize for the former untruthful statements, you seek another issue. . . . Your first charge was that I was connected with an attempt to bribe the attorney general of Ohio nine years ago, but that you have abandoned . . . Charles P. Taft, brother of your candidate, in his *Ohio State Journal* of Columbus, says: 'There has been no evidence produced against Haskell that would be considered by any court.' It remains for you alone to lack the manhood to candidly admit that you accuse me falsely."

When Haskell was sued for a $1,200 hotel bill at Muskogee, the *Oklahoma City Times* rubbed salt in the wounds by starting a public subscription to pay the "board bill." Several contributors identified as Republicans sent in amounts ranging from a penny to a nickel.

Throughout the fall campaign, rumors spread of a renewed investigation into the town lot sales at Muskogee in 1901. In making allotments to the Creek Indians, the government had decreed that an individual owning a town lot could buy another at half the appraised price. Haskell, then president of the Southern Trading and Contracting Co., was building a railroad from Fayetteville. Muskogee citizens had given the right-of-way into the city and a $6,000 subsidy, but in the transaction was a number of lots which M. L. Mott, an attorney for the Creeks, later charged had been acquired through "dummy" purchasers.

Haskell knew that Sylvester Rush, an Omaha lawyer, had been sent to Oklahoma to assist in the government's investigation, and he charged privately that Roosevelt was out to "get" him. What he didn't know, and what comes to light now for the first time in proper sequence, is a letter the president sent to his attorney general on Nov. 2, 1908. It read:

"I should like to have some man specially detailed to consult with the Interior Department and go down to Oklahoma and find out if there is not some way of bringing Governor Haskell to speedy justice. I think him one of the most corrupt blackguards that has drifted to the top in any place in our American political life. If he could be put in stripes it would be an admirable thing for the cause of decent government."

For several days, Samuel McReynolds, a New York lawyer, had been in Guthrie gathering evidence for William Randolph Hearst for use in defending against Haskell's pending slander and libel suit. The governor had McReynolds arrested in the capitol (courthouse) on January 19, charging that the lawyer "has been offering large sums to aid in manufacturing false statements." A sheaf of papers McReynolds was carrying was impounded.

Roosevelt's demand for action culminated in a federal grand jury investigation of the lot frauds at Muskogee. On Feb. 3, 1909, the jury returned indictments against Haskell and six other prominent men, including Col. F. B. Severs (for whom the Severs hotel was named) and Haskell's friend, C. W. Turner, for whom he named the Turner building. Haskell promptly issued a statement saying he was satisfied "the interior department has been misled by false statements. I am confident there has not been a dishonest act done by any of the indicted parties."

More than 20 lawyers, Republicans and Democrats, offered their services to the governor, among them Henry Asp and A. C. Cruce. The latter was a brother of Lee Cruce. Before he and Mrs. Haskell left Guthrie the night of the fourth, a delegation of prominent Guthrie citizens called to present Haskell with a bond for $5,000. It had been signed by 27 men whose aggregate wealth was approximately $1,250,000. Of the signers, 14 were Republicans.

At Muskogee, the Haskells were met at the train with a band and the crowd, estimated by Muskogee reporters at 500, grew in size to about 2,000 by the time they reached the hotel.

"Every accused person is entitled to the benefit of the doubt," declared Bryan, at Lincoln, "but in the case of the governor of Oklahoma, it is particularly true . . . in any federal proceedings brought against him. This is so because Governor Haskell was long ago marked for slaughter by the president of the United States."

The indictment, charging conspiracy to defraud, was quashed in a hearing at Tulsa on April 10 on a technicality; the grand jury had consisted of 21 men, instead of 16, under a new legal interpretation. W. J. Gregg, the U. S. district attorney, presented the case before a new grand jury at Tulsa in May.

Before John A. Marshall, a federal judge from Salt Lake City assigned to hear the case, Gregg called for discharge of the jury on May 15. He declared the jurors were ignoring evidence produced by "creditable witnesses" and that the jury was under improper influence.

"Without expressing my opinion as to the conduct of this grand jury, the court will discharge it from further service at this time, and the clerk will be directed to call a grand jury from the body of the district exclusive of Muskogee county," Judge Marshall announced. The new jury was impaneled three days later and promptly voted new indictments.

Defense attacks on the indictments were overruled by Judge Marshall in November, 1909, but the case dragged on for months. Following a circuit court ruling in a similar case from Wyoming in June, 1910, the charges were dismissed in a final hearing at McAlester. The Wyoming case held that, under the statute of limitations, the government must show some continuing act within three years of the indictment. In Haskell's case eight years had elapsed before the first indictment.

CHAPTER IX

A Sacrifice to Politics?

MEANTIME, the Depositors' Guaranty Fund was in the news again. On August 8, 1908, U. S. Attorney General Charles J. Bonaparte advised the comptroller of the currency that it would be illegal for national banks to participate in the plan. Fifty-seven national banks had come into the program voluntarily under provisions of Section 4. In his legal ruling, Bonaparte commented there had been discussion as to whether the guaranty plan "can be considered an insurance of the bank's deposits and, as such, a legitimate, if somewhat novel, feature in the conduct of its business."

But he held that "the business of insuring deposits is a wholly separate business from that of banking, and a corporation organized for the latter business would have no greater right to embarrass its funds and risk its credit in the former than it would have to engage in life insurance or fire insurance or casualty or marine insurance." He added since it would be illegal for officers of a national bank to enter into "such agreement as contemplated by Section 4 . . . persistent and wilful action to this effect on the part of any such bank would be just cause for the forfeiture of its charter."

Forced to choose, some of the 57 national banks withdrew from the guaranty system while others elected to surrender their national charters and convert to state banks. On September 11, the state supreme court in the Noble State bank case upheld the law as constitutional in a unanimous decision. Chief Justice Williams wrote the opinion brushing aside the contention that the levy to maintain the fund amounted to taking property without due process of law.

"What are banks organized for?" he asked. "Are the officers and stockholders acting from a spirit of philanthrophy in securing a charter and establishing such business? Or is it done for the purpose of gain? * * *

"Each bank having a reciprocal interest in the Depositors' Guaranty Fund, then each has an incidental reciprocal interest in every other bank. The bank can no more properly be permitted to say in regard to other banks, 'Am I my brother's keeper?' than could the man in Holy Writ in the days of old, in the sight of Jehovah, repeat with approval such a subterfuge, for under this law each banker is his brother's keeper; he having an individual interest in the result of the management of each bank . . . and there should be enough of the milk of human kindness in the soul of every man, whether he be banker, money lender, farmer or laborer, that he should take pleasure in participating in the reimbursement of losses occasioned by such misfortune."

The Noble bank appealed to the United States supreme court where, months later, in a memorable decision by Justice Oliver Wendell Holmes, that tribunal also upheld the law. Said Justice Holmes, in an opinion handed down in January, 1911:

"The only contract it (the Noble bank) relies upon is its charter. That is subject to alteration or repeal, as usual, so that the obligation hardly could be said to be impaired by the act of 1907 before us. . . .

"The substance of the plaintiff's argument is that the assessment takes private property for private use without compensation. And while we should assume that the plaintiff would retain a reversionary interest in the contribution to the fund, so as to be entitled to a return of what remained of it if the purpose were given up, still there is no denying that by this law a portion of its property might be taken without return, to pay debts of a failing rival in business. Nevertheless, notwithstanding the logical form of the objection, there are more powerful considerations on the other side.

"In the first place, it is established by a series of cases that an ulterior public advantage may justify a comparatively insignificant taking of private property for what, in its immediate purpose, is a private use. And in the next, it would seem that there may be other cases besides the every-day one of taxation, in which the share to each party in the benefit of a scheme of mutual protection is sufficient compensation for the correlative burden that it is compelled to assume.

"At least, if we have a case within the reasonable exercise of the police power, as above explained, no more need be said . . . We cannot say that the public interests to which we have adverted, and others, are not sufficient to warrant the state in taking the whole business of banking under its control. On the contrary, we are of the opinion that it may go on from regulation to prohibition except upon such conditions as it may prescribe. In short, when the Oklahoma legislature declares by implication that free banking is a public danger, and that incorporation, inspection, and the above-described cooperation are necessary safeguards, this court cannot say that is wrong."

There were repercussions, meantime, from closing the International bank at Coalgate. In an interview with the *Oklahoma City Times* on Sept. 4, 1908, Dr. L. A. Conner, the bank's president, declared:

"I will never believe anything else but that my bank was closed by Bank Commissioner Smock on telephone orders from Governor Haskell, for no other purpose than to make a demonstration for the Depositors' Guaranty law for the Democratic convention at Denver." He said less than $500 was needed from the fund to pay off depositors, and citing the bank's statements for Feb. 15, 1908, and May 21, the day of closing, Dr. Conner added:

"It will be noted that the condition of the bank, at the time its doors were closed, according to the above statements, shows a much healthier condition when the doors were closed than when the guaranty license was issued three months previous. The question naturally arises, why should the bank be closed? An illustration of the workings of the law was necessary for campaign purposes. The author of the law was sure that he would be in a position at Denver to make his pet scheme a national issue in the presidential campaign now in progress, and he needed something to point to with pride."

Dr. Conner and the bank's cashier were under bail following arrest for violating the banking laws, the charges being based on about $11,000 in personal notes among the bank's assets. When the matter was laid before a grand jury at Ada in October, the jury refused to indict the bank officials and censured Smock instead. Its report read, in part:

"From the testimony of Mr. Smock himself, this bank was solvent when it was closed by the state, and to add to the inconsistency of all the transactions in connection with this affair, an abundance of proof was before the grand jury that the bank was in better condition when it was closed than when it became a state institution and was permitted to partake of all the benefits and privileges of the state guaranty law. And notwithstanding the knowledge of this, and contrary to the statutes of Oklahoma, Mr. Smock permitted this institution to continue to do business as a state bank . . . in direct violation of Section 8, Article II, of House Bill 615 passed the last session of the state legislature."

The jury recommended Smock's removal and that the evidence be brought to the attention of the next grand jury. Indignantly, Smock denied the charges.

"I am surprised that any body of men of average intelligence could be so grossly misled," he asserted. "They are either ignorant or have purposely disregarded the facts in the case in order to slap the guaranty law in the heat of a political campaign. . . .

"So far as my action in closing the bank is concerned, I have no apologies to make and will follow the same course again should it become necessary. I am a Republican and am certainly not running this office to make political thunder for the Democratic party . . . The facts in the Coalgate case are plain, as the records will show, and there is no question but that the officers of the bank were guilty of wilfully and knowingly violating the provisions of the banking laws."

Smock, a carryover from the territorial administration, tendered his resignation November 3, however, to become second vice president of the Columbia Bank & Trust Co. of Oklahoma City. In a general reorganization, W. L. Norton, of Bartlesville, who headed the American National bank in that city, became president of the Columbia. Under the stimulus of guaranteed deposits, the Columbia reported in a newspaper advertisement on December 5 an increase in deposits from $347,756 on July 15 to $602,592 on November 27.

That was only the beginning of a spectacular spiral which would zoom the Columbia in less than a year to the largest bank in the state, in point of deposits. It was a spiral which would threaten to wreck the Depositors' Guaranty Fund—but that was still in the future.

In September, Haskell appointed the three judges to the Criminal Court of Appeals. Created by the first legislature to relieve the supreme court from having to consider appeals in criminal cases, it was to function until Jan. 1, 1911, or until the law was repealed. It is still in existence, of course. Chosen for presiding judge was Henry M. Furman of Ada, the unsung hero among the Democrats for his gallantry in the U. S. senate race. Then, Haskell fashion, the governor selected Thomas H. Doyle of Perry, one of his primary opponents of the year before, for another of the appointments. The third went to H. G. Baker of Muskogee.

In November, Bryan carried Oklahoma, but the margin of less than 20,000 was disappointing. Taft swept the nation. A Republican would be in the White House another four years, but with Democrats holding a reduced but impressive majority in the legislature, Senator Gore was assured a new full six-year term. When first elected to the senate the year before, the Lawton man received the short term by lot, thereby necessitating a second campaign in 1908.

CHAPTER X

Kate Barnard Rescues the Convicts

THE smoke from the November election had hardly cleared away before Haskell was facing public clamor for removal of Oklahoma's convicts from the "hell hole" of the Kansas penitentiary at Lansing. Since Oklahoma territory was without a state prison, the territory had contracted with Kansas to keep its convicts. The contract, continued at the outset of the Haskell administration, called for payment of 40 cents a day per prisoner. In addition, Kansas had the privilege of working the convicts in prison coal mines or assigning them to contractors operating furniture and twine factories within the walls.

Indian territory, on the other hand, had sent its convicts to federal prisons, but with statehood, felons from that section also were sent to Lansing.

In August, 1908, Miss Kate Barnard, commissioner of charities and corrections, decided to investigate the mounting complaints of cruel treatment and deplorable conditions in the Lansing prison. A spirited Irish girl from Nebraska, Miss Barnard had followed her father to Oklahoma territory two years after the opening. With a warm heart for the unfortunate, she entered welfare work at an early age and by the time of the Constitutional Convention, she was well known to public officials in Oklahoma City and Guthrie. She was the "darling" of the farm and labor delegates in the convention, a close friend of Pete Hanraty, a vice president, and it was said the office of Commissioner of Charities and Corrections "was made for Kate Barnard."

Denied the right to vote herself, this young woman of only 31 years led the state ticket in 1907—polling about 500 votes more than Haskell!

Upon her return, Miss Barnard reported privately to Haskell on her Lansing visit, but the governor had his hands full with campaign problems and it is probable that he persuaded her to hold up her published report until after the November election. Then it broke in full fury in the newspapers on December 11.

"My coming was not heralded, and in company with the general crowd of visitors, I paid the usual admittance fee, and with them was shown through what the prisoners called the 'show places of the prison,'" she wrote, and Miss Barnard knew how to write! "I did this to get my bearings. I returned to the office and presented my card, saying that my business at the prison was to make a thorough investigation. My request caused the greatest surprise and consternation.

"Warden Haskell (not related to Governor Haskell) questioned my right to inspect the prison as an officer of the state of Oklahoma, but very courteously offered to show me over the institution as a private citizen. The board of control was in session that day. One member said:

"'I would like to know who commissioned you to come here and spy upon this institution.' I replied, 'I am commissioned by a million and a half Oklahoma citizens to investigate this penitentiary. Either show me through as a state officer of Oklahoma, or order me out. I shall do my duty here, unless I am forced from this institution.'"

Warden Haskell finally yielded, and Miss Barnard continued her report:

"I spent several hours down in the mines, visited the punishment chamber, saw the 'crib' which had been many times explained to me by released prisoners, saw the dungeons, saw where the 'water cure' was administered and, on September 7, made a written report to the governor containing substantially what I am now relating to you."

At the time, there were 562 men and 13 women prisoners from Oklahoma at Lansing. When prison officials persisted in hamstringing her efforts, Miss Barnard said, "I told Warden Haskell most emphatically that I proposed to interview all the Oklahoma men. When he saw I was determined, he reluctantly offered to allow me to speak to such as I would designate, in his private office."

The plucky young commissioner decided to visit the coal mines.

"I, myself, as small as I am, had to get down and crawl through many of these passages where, if the roof would give ever so little, a large man could never get by. One Oklahoma boy told me, with tear-streaming eyes, that he was frightened to death to work in this mine, that he had been called upon to pull three men out from under the falling slate in the last year.

"Another young man from Oklahoma told me that they put him

in the mine the day he came, that he knew nothing about digging coal, and that two or three times he 'set the gas off' and was constantly afraid of an explosion. One of the worst features of this mine is that the prisoners have what they call a 'stunt'; in other words, a certain day's work to perform. This work consists of mining three cars of coal a day.

"This law is as inexorable as fate itself. Whatever happens, those three cars must come, and I found one little 17-year-old boy—from Oklahoma—locked up in a black dungeon, shackled to a sprocket in the wall, because he was unable to extract from the inky depths those three cars of coal. He told me with tears in his eyes, that he could not get out any more, that the coal was so hard and that he had never dug any coal before and he did not know how to dig it," her report continued.

"Several prisoners complained of the 'water hole' and the 'crib.' While I was in the mine, the superintendent went forward to speak to a guard when a coal-begrimed convict shot swiftly, silently and stealthily from the darkness, grabbed me by the arm and whispered these words: 'See the water hole, girl, for God's sake, see the water hole.'

"I said, 'What is the water hole?' He answered, 'Where they throw us in and pump water on us. It's terrible; see it.' Before I had time to ask where to find the water hole, the convict was gone—the superintendent was returning. Later I was passing a bunch of prisoners with the superintendent considerably in the lead, when another prisoner leaned cautiously forward and hurriedly warned me to 'see the water hole.'

"I asked the warden an hour later; he answered, 'there is no water hole.' Two weeks after my return from Lansing, I received the following letter from one of the prisoners there, but withhold the name of the prisoner lest the fury of the authorities fall heavily on his hapless head:

"' * * * I am an Oklahoma prisoner and my work has permitted me to study the inside. Your coming was as a bolt of thunder from a clear sky and you shook this rotten old institution with the first genuine scare they have had since the time of the Populists. But do not be deceived—you only scared them temporarily. After you had come and gone we fell into the old rut and by Saturday night, the 'holes' were all full and the 'crib' and water played no small part, so official displeasure at your frankly-expressed opinions vented itself in retaliation upon helpless convicts.

"'When you announced yourself, the whitewash was quickly applied wherever possible before your coming so you only saw a part—a small part. We all wonder if you will ever learn the whole truth * * * Already we have learned to call you, not jestingly, but reverently, "Our Kate," for your coming, while it has as yet borne no fruit but thorns, was to us as the sudden appearance of a light house in a stormy sea—a rose in a desert waste.' "

Still insistent, Miss Barnard said she finally found "in the hall of punishments something called the 'crib.' The 'crib' is a coffin-like structure, constructed of slats, about the size of a man. They throw a man into this 'crib' and lock the lid on him. This was intended originally to be sufficient punishment.

"I am told by an Oklahoma prisoner who has been in the Lansing penitentiary that they shackle the hands and feet of a man, draw them in a knot at his back and then throw him into this 'crib' and lock the lid down. This punishment caused temporary paralysis to one prisoner. Warden Haskell tells me that he has not allowed this since his charge of the prison. However, an Oklahoma prisoner, whose name I am prepared to give, stated to me in the presence of Warden Haskell, that as a punishment to him Warden Haskell had thrown him into this 'crib' and strapped him down with his back to the bottom of the structure, had shackled his hands with handcuffs, and then ordered the guard to turn the garden hose on his nostrils and mouth until his head and lungs were filled with water almost to a point of suffocation.

"Warden Haskell heard this man tell this, and acknowledged it. This, I believe, is cruel and inhuman and unnecessary punishment and too obsolete to be inflicted in a twentieth century Christian civilization."

On the second day of her visit, Miss Barnard said she found a 17-year-old Oklahoman shackled to the dungeon wall who had asked to see the warden. Under prison rules, the guard was supposed to report the boy's request to the warden, but had not done so.

"I took it upon myself to reprimand the guard, and went immediately to the warden with the case," Miss Barnard added.

She said prisoners in the mines complained of hunger. She quoted an official report that Kansas spent 10.9 cents a day per man for food.

"The dinner which was served to the miners while I was in the mine consisted of two pieces of bologna sausage, three inches long, with all the prisoners wanted of plain bread and tomato and pea soup." She pointed out that Oklahoma paid 40 cents a day for each prisoner, under the contract with Kansas, while Kansas furnished the prison clothing.

"This probably brings the total average cost of maintenance up to 48 cents per capita for each day," she added, "but the state of Kansas in addition had the profits from cheap labor for the furniture and twine factory contractors and labor in the coal mines." Miss Barnard said she thought it a mistake "in putting convicts in mines at all, because a convict mine tends to deaden and brutalize, and these men need such work as will reclaim them."

But she did not spare Oklahoma lawmakers, either. In concluding her report, she wrote:

"Now while I am arraigning the bad points of this institution, I feel that there is something for which we ourselves are terribly to blame, a condition which, thank God, is not due to our administration, but was bequeathed to us from lawless conditions which were maintained in the territory.

"From August, 1905, to the present time, sixty little boys under 17 years of age have been incarcerated in the Lansing penitentiary—from Oklahoma! Think of the Saviour that took little children into his arms and blessed them. What would we answer if He were to return now to the Lansing penitentiary and ask us Oklahomans, 'What are my little ones doing here?' "

Miss Barnard investigated the federal jail at McAlester, where it was proposed to house Oklahoma's worst offenders, and found the building "utterly unsuited for keeping such a large body of men." With regard to plans for the new penitentiary, she concluded:

"There are prisons and prisons. Both have locks and bars, but there is every difference in the world between them. I hope for the credit of the state, that only the best standards will be chosen."

Publication of the report brought indignant denials from the Kansas warden, who declared Miss Barnard had "slandered" the prison officials. He said it was necessary "to hold unruly prisoners in check, but such tortures and 'wild-eyed' stories emanating from Guthrie 'dope shops' are absolutely without foundation." Three days later, Governor Haskell said he had not read the report, but added:

"Miss Barnard is a good woman, and a good, industrious official, and has a heart full of sympathy for the unfortunate, and her kindness of heart would make things look cruel to her that an ordinary citizen would consider proper and necessary."

Nevertheless, public reaction forced Gov. Edward W. Hoch of

Kansas to appoint an investigating committee, and J. P. Connors hurried up to Lansing to have a look. Connors, president of the state board of agriculture, was one of the three members of the new prison board of control. The other members were Haskell and Attorney General West.

The first legislature had appropriated $50,000 for the new penitentiary, and to bring the Oklahoma convicts back to the state. When Charles E. N. Coles, the first prison superintendent, died suddenly on November 5 during a visit to Guthrie, the governor looked for a capable successor. He had heard of an aggressive mayor of Ardmore who, despite local opposition, had taken the bull by the horns to install a modern water works and other improvements. Also, he was a friend of Lee Cruce, Haskell's primary opponent, who had been drawn into the governor's official family as chairman of the university board of regents. Haskell placed a long distance call to R. W. Dick and offered him appointment as warden.

R. W. Dick
Ardmore mayor appointed to build prison and move convicts.

When Dick accepted, the governor sent him to McAlester to hasten construction of a barbed wire enclosure with temporary barracks to contain the convicts while the prisoners themselves were employed in building the walls and cell blocks of the new penitentiary.

Returning from Lansing December 23, Connors declared, "Kate is right in her assertions, and she has not told half the horrors of some of the punishments."

At Haskell's direction, Dick obtained the use of "Old Spot Ten," a passenger coach with steel bars over the windows and steel doors, to begin moving the convicts in groups of 50. The coach had been equipped by the Katy for carrying federal prisoners. Oklahoma's contract with Kansas would expire on Jan. 31, 1909. When the new legislature convened in early January, there was renewed agitation to speed up the removal of Oklahoma's prisoners, and bills went into the hopper to prevent the abuses cited by Miss Barnard. One bill, by Sen. W. N. Redwine of McAlester, forbade the use of convicts as contract labor—and it's still the law.

On January 28, the prison board chartered a special train of seven coaches and dispatched Dick and Connors, with some 25 or 30 sheriffs and deputies, to Lansing to complete the removal. Twenty years later, Dick would relate some of the experiences of that memorable journey in an interview with Alvin Rucker, *The Oklahoman's* roving correspondent:

"It was a joyous event in the lives of the convicts when they marched out of Lansing penitentiary and began the return trip to Oklahoma. To the convicts, the journey meant 'going home,' as they expressed it in shouts, laughter and song. A terrific blizzard was raging when the convicts marched out of the Lansing penitentiary building, and that facilitated getting them safely aboard the train, for they welcomed the warmth of the passenger coaches.

"We placed them, two in a seat, with each convict being shackled to a long chain. It took a long time to get them aboard the train and properly fixed in seats, and as a result the train did not start until after noon. When the wheels finally began to turn, rolling the train southward, the silence that had pervaded gave way to shouts of joy and singing."

Dick wired ahead to Kansas City for 5,000 sandwiches and barrels of coffee.

"When we reached Kansas City, the sandwiches and coffee were loaded into a baggage coach, and from then on I tried to keep the convicts so busy eating they would have no time for planning outbreaks," he related. Dick's plan was to keep the train moving—thus lessening any chance for escape—until he reached Vinita, where some of the more dangerous prisoners were lodged in the federal jail. But the warden wanted to arrive at McAlester in daylight and the train crew was traveling on "orders." Since their "orders" would put the train in McAlester at night, the warden staged his own "train holdup" —sending armed guards to detain the engine crew. Thus relieved of their "orders," they stalled the train.

At McAlester, the hastily-built stockade was ready. When Dick accepted Haskell's appointment, he persuaded F. W. Broadnax, superintendent of the water and sewer department at Ardmore, to take charge of construction. Broadnax had strung strands of barbed wire at a distance around the barracks, and the wire was charged with electricity.

Dick advised the convicts of this lethal charge, but many were skeptical. One day a prisoner came into contact with the wire and was electrocuted. That set off an investigation by a joint committee of the third legislature, which exonerated Dick.

The committee reported the death "was purely accidental, and due to the carelessness of the prisoner himself. The evidence shows that the prisoner was running an empty wheelbarrow through the gateway to the fence, said gateway being about 10 feet wide, with ample room for him to pass without being in any danger, but owing to his carelessness, he ran the wheelbarrow against the fence and the fatal result followed."

"News travels rapidly among prisoners," Dick related, "and soon all were convinced that the fence was an instrument of death."

On Jan. 5, 1909, Haskell greeted the second legislature with this message:

"Our state of Oklahoma has completed its first year under state government and we have reason to express our gratification for its progress and the fact that its occasional misfortunes are far outweighed by its general prosperity."

He boasted of "the remarkable record" made by state banks under the guaranty fund. He cited first the deposit record:

National banks on Dec. 3, 1907, had $38,316,729 in individual deposits; on Nov. 27, 1908, $36,280,346, a decrease of $2,038,383.

State banks, on the other hand, showed an increase from $17,215,535 on Dec. 15, 1907, to $29,448,070 on Nov. 27, 1908, a gain of $12,233,435. Parenthetically, he added that "it's fair to say that about 30 national banks reorganized as state banks during the year, which substantially accounts for nearly all of the $2,000,000" decline in deposits in the national bank total.

"Out of a total of over 500 state banks," Haskell added, "there has not been a single failure during the year, and only one small bank closed and that was for gross violation of the state banking law—the violation consisting of managing officers borrowing the funds deposited in the bank, and upon failure to comply with the bank commissioner's order to replace the borrowed money, the bank was closed; the depositors paid within 48 hours, and within less than three months, the department had liquidated this bank to the point where the draft on the State Guaranty Fund had been entirely replaced, and assets remaining, equivalent to about 55 percent for the stockholders.

"We congratulate the people of our state on the success of its banking law and commend the banking department of the state upon its vigilant and efficient discharge or management of that department, and the bank officers upon the assistance they have rendered the department in making the banking business safe and generally satisfactory to the people."

As an indication the guaranty fund was attracting deposits from out-of-state, the governor offered congratulations "to our people on the stable condition produced in banking circles, the confidence and approval of the people, not only within our state, but in two-thirds of the other states of the Union whose people have added to the deposits of the Oklahoma state banks." Unwittingly, the governor had put his finger on a facet which would produce the year's biggest headache—the collapse of the state's largest banking institution.

Blind Tom Gore, who had drawn the short term in the United States senate the year before, was unopposed in the Democratic preferential primary in 1908 and while the Republicans recorded substantial gains in the legislature, Democrats still held overwhelming control. Gore was re-elected formally on January 20, winning over Dennis Flynn, the Republican choice.

It was a day when good spirits prevailed, and Flynn added his bit with this dry remark when invited to address the joint session:

"By your votes, you have decided that Mr. Gore shall buy a ticket for Washington, and that I shall buy one for Oklahoma City."

CHAPTER XI

Institutional Bloc and a Bank Crash

IN his first message to the second legislature, Haskell declared "Your public officers have had, beyond question, the most difficult undertaking ever experienced in the organization of a new state.

"The unusual experience of forming one state out of two territories widely differing in territorial laws and conditions would, of itself, present many difficulties, but when we contemplate that one of these great territories had no territorial form of government, no county, no township or school district organizations, that 40 counties carved out of that unorganized territory began their county government on the day of statehood—that not one of these 40 counties had any organization or money to conduct their business; that the entire first year of statehood, and more, would have to elapse before there could be any cash in the county or district treasuries, other than borrowed money . . . Oklahoma asks its own people as well as the people of other states of the Union, and the world at large, to judge our state, our people and our laws from the truth of conditions, rather than from criticism and unreliable reports. Let the facts speak for themselves!"

Briefly, he reviewed department reports reflecting the material prosperity of the state: Farm products, $201,416,805, an increase of $13,083,201 over the previous year; $6,130,872 in coal production, $2,384,084 in lead and zinc, and $20,688,756 in oil.

"This does not include the value upon the natural gas production," he continued, "which has been equal to 140 billion cubic feet, and amounts to 7,750 tons of coal . . . The very fact that this gas can be had in many localities at 3 cents per 1,000 cubic feet, or even less, affords the most attractive inducements for manufacturing concerns to locate within our state . . . The policy of our government from the beginning has been to retain our natural gas for consumption within the state. Three distinct efforts during the year have been made to create an interstate pipeline to convey Oklahoma gas to outside points. We have successfully defeated these several efforts. . . ."

With gubernatorial restraint removed, the second legislature plunged into the delectable task of creating new state institutions. Oklahoma territory had the University, the A. and M. college and normal schools at Edmond, Alva and Weatherford from territorial days, and the preparatory school at Tonkawa. Legislators from the old Indian territory section were particularly aggressive in the new effort to "balance up" the institutions already established.

The upshot was the formation of a voting clique in the legislature —composed of senators and representatives from the counties with state institutions—that became known as the "institutional bloc." Its influence is still felt in the legislature when the subject of appropriations is under discussion.

After a sharp fight in the house, Rep. W. A. Durant succeeded in substituting his home town of Durant for Ada in locating the Southeast normal, although the original $100,000 appropriation request for buildings was cut to $25,000. Haskell was instrumental in getting the Northeast Normal located at Tahlequah where the state acquired the old Cherokee Female Seminary.

The first legislature had authorized an Industrial Institute and College for Girls, but without appropriation or location. In large newspaper ads, Claremore, "the garden spot of Rogers county," and Chickasha, "with advantages unequalled," paraded their civic charms before the lawmakers.

When Chickasha finally won the school, Claremore was given the Eastern Oklahoma Preparatory school (offsetting the Tonkawa institution). It was an exciting day in the house when Chickasha won the girls' school (now Oklahoma College for Women). With the roll call 64 to 36, a delegation of Chickasha women broke into cheers. An enterprising reporter, intrigued with the enthusiasm of an attractive young woman in green, learned she was Mrs. Ed Johns, wife of a Chickasha business man.

The bill carried $100,000 for a building, but as in the case of other new educational institutions, nothing was appropriated for salaries. It was necessary for the local communities to raise operating funds by local subscription.

The Granite "secondary penitentiary" bill passed the house in February with an appropriation of $50,000. The State Training school —originally for both boys and girls—was located between Pauls Valley and Wynnewood in March.

Sen. Reuben M. Roddie, an administration supporter who had

written the Depositors' Guaranty Fund bill in the first legislature, finally got through a bill creating a normal school for Ada—now East Central. The first president was Charles W. Briles, who had a long career in educational work. An early faculty member was W. D. Little who later became publisher of the *Ada Evening News,* and chairman of the board of regents for higher education.

Little, a native of North Carolina, went to Sulphur in 1908. He taught the first year at Palmer, a rural school, but when East Central was established in 1909, he was elected head of the English department. "That was before much scholarship was required of professors," he wryly confessed later.

Among his students were Grady Mathews, later state health commissioner; Robert S. Kerr, destined to become Oklahoma's first native-born governor and later U. S. senator; Wilburn Cartwright, later congressman and presently corporation commissioner; Harvey Black and Harry Simmons, prominent in education, and Miss Muriel Wright, one of the state's outstanding historians.

"So you can see of that small bunch of boys and girls, some rather famous ones have remained," Little wrote in 1957.

Sen. George O. Johnson of Fort Cobb was asphyxiated in his sleep on Feb. 10, 1909, and Sen. P. J. Yeager, Tulsa, his roommate, narrowly escaped death.

Roddie offered amendments to the original banking law increasing capital requirements for state banks. On a population basis, the minimum requirements were increased to $15,000 in cities of 1,500 or less, $50,000 in cities of 6,000 to 10,000, and $100,000 in cities of over 10,000. Also, the law made it a misdemeanor for a bank to advertise deposits "guaranteed by the state;" it was permissible, however, to advertise that deposits were protected by the guaranty fund.

The guaranty fund received its most critical test in September when the Columbia Bank & Trust Co. of Oklahoma City, the largest bank in the state, was placed in the hands of the bank commissioner.

"We congratulate the people of our state on the success of its banking law," Haskell had told the legislature in January. Now the governor, with customary vigor, moved in to take personal charge. Haskell's first bank commissioner, H. H. Smock, had resigned in November, 1908, to become second vice president of the Columbia when W. L. Norton, a genial financier not above personal speculation in oil and real estate, became president.

Within a year, deposits skyrocketed from $365,686 on Sept. 23, 1908, to a record $2,806,008 on Sept. 1, 1909. Yet when the state took over on the night of Sept. 28, 1909, there was only about $28,000 cash in the till and $185,000 in sight exchange. Fortunately for Haskell and the guaranty fund, individual deposits were only about one-third the total. Even so, the guaranty fund amounted to about $300,000, of which $50,000 was deposited in the Columbia bank.

Some of the deposits were worthy of note. J. A. "Sunny Jim" Menefee, the state treasurer, was a stockholder and as state treasurer had $189,165.10 in the bank on September 28. That was $61,782 more than he had on deposit there the first of the month, and it revealed one method by which Columbia deposits had soared.

The commissioner of the land office had $190,000 on deposit when the bank closed, and 119 out-of-city banks had accounts totaling $1,328,383. State deposits were secured, of course, by securities, but the lack of availability of these pledged securities made Haskell's problem to raise quick cash the more difficult. Individual deposits stood at $1,081,898 on September 27, and the Norton management from the outset had conducted an intensive campaign to entice new deposits —both in Oklahoma and from outside the state—with advertisements offering 4 percent interest with all deposits protected by the guaranty fund.

In his exhaustive study of the Guaranty Fund in 1920, Robb traced the manipulations of Norton and his associates which sapped the bank's resources. For some time, the comptroller of the currency had been suspicious of the oil paper held by national banks in Oklahoma.

"Alarmed by the conditions in the oil business, he sent special examiners into eastern Oklahoma with instructions to charge off suspicious paper whether it was due or not," Robb wrote. "The result was that most of the paper of Norton and his associates was thrown out of the national banks.

"This paper, ejected from the national banks, now began to appear thick and fast at the Columbia bank. During August and September, over $648,000 of this oil paper was dumped on the Columbia. When the Columbia failed, it had an overdraft account of $189,000, most of these overdrafts being against companies in which W. L. Norton was interested. The strain was more than the resources of the Columbia could stand."

Robb reported that among the uncollected assets after liquidation were five personal notes of Norton for $211,563.

First public intimation that the bank was in difficulty was a newspaper story the morning of September 28, reporting a rumor that Menefee would succeed Norton as president. Hurrying down from Guthrie, Haskell went into conference with Menefee, Smock, A. M. Young, his new bank commissioner; I. M. Putnam, legislator and real estate promoter (disclosed later as owing the bank $60,520) and W. T. Kemper, a Kansas City banker. *The Oklahoman* reported Haskell was "not inclined to be very communicative," but the governor said he had been in conference with a view to making Oklahoma City a reserve center for state banks.

But the next day came announcement that the affairs of the Columbia were in the hands of the state "which will pay its depositors dollar for dollar upon demand." Roy Oakes, secretary of the state banking board, advised depositors: "Bring your books and, in cases of mutual account, be ready to present claims. Contested or disputed claims will also receive prompt attention."

Norton attempted to reassure depositors with this statement:

"False rumors circulated, causing unusual withdrawals from our bank, which made the state deem it best to temporarily take charge of the bank until all matters can be properly adjusted. This will be done in a very short time, as we consider the assets more than sufficient to meet all obligations."

Haskell sized up the situation quickly and moved into action. As the night's long conference dragged on, the governor opened long distance lines to Kansas City and St. Louis where he had influential banker friends. He arranged for a $250,000 cash advance from each city, to be secured by collateral from the Columbia. When Commissioner Young expressed some hesitancy about opening in the morning to pay depositors before he had a chance to check the bank's records and securities, Haskell advised him to go to bed and get a good night's sleep.

"But see me in the morning before 8:30," the governor added, "so I'll have time to appoint a new bank commissioner if you don't open for business."

The state board authorized a special levy of ¾ of 1 percent against deposits in state banks to meet the emergency.

Promptly at 9 next morning, Young opened the bank. W. A. Ledbetter, the governor's crony from the Constitutional Convention, was on hand to assist. The crowd was smaller than anticipated, but Ledbetter mounted a table to get their attention. These two were putting up a bold front while Haskell played for time.

"We have discovered some inaccuracies in the books," Ledbetter told the depositors. "So, to avoid future trouble, I shall require each of you to bring your bank book and sign an affidavit that your bank book is correct."

Fred S. Barde, the veteran *Kansas City Star* correspondent, wired his paper:

"Stacks of bags filled with gold and silver and piles of currency were in the cage of the paying teller, James Walley. One of the state inspectors, W. A. Ledbetter, was beside Bank Commissioner Young as his adviser.

"When the doors of the marble entrance of the bank swung open, fewer than 100 persons were waiting for admittance and 10 minutes later the sidewalk in front of the bank was easily passable. At 9:30, there were probably 150 depositors in line inside the bank, and of this number not to exceed 10 percent were women.

"Mrs. L. Mathewson of Oklahoma City was the first person to ask for withdrawal of her deposit. She was paid $120, the full amount she had in the bank. By 9:37 o'clock, only three depositors had been paid, time and care being required to make proofs of claims. One of these deposits was for $1,000."

The Oklahoman on September 30 reported:

"The much-heralded 'run' on the bank yesterday dwindled to nothing by noon, and that none might be disappointed who wished to withdraw funds, the doors were kept open until 5 p. m., instead of 3 p. m., as usual." In a statement dictated for the papers, Haskell blamed "a few national bankers" for persistent criticism but said "the vast majority are courteous and fair with their state bank neighbors."

"The people met on every hand are expressing satisfaction with the peaceful, orderly way with which the state law of Oklahoma settles these difficulties without loss to the people. We find the Columbia Bank & Trust Co. condition stronger after a day's active investigation than appeared to us the night before we took charge. . . . We have to warn the people of the state against fake and malicious news items as the enemy of the state law circulate, the latest of which is an alleged special from Guthrie to the effect that state bankers have agreed to resist payment of an emergency assessment. The state of Oklahoma has always been fair to both classes of banks, and national banks today have on deposit over $1,000,000 of state money which could at once be transferred if the state were disposed to be unfriendly to the national banks."

By Thursday the governor was predicting the bank would be turned back to its officers on Monday.

"The Oklahoma banking law is a complete success, even against the persistent opposition of a strong element of other classes of bankers," he said. "We adjust the affairs of an embarrassed state bank with perfect ease in a very few days, and with no public clamor whatever. Everybody is in good humor and conditions are normal. Depositors' money was not tied up a single hour. Other state banks are quiet and gaining in deposits."

Haskell was talking a good game. During the first day, Columbia depositors were paid $228,000. Individuals were being paid, but the banks which had deposits tied up were forced to wait. When Attorney General West intimated he would ask a grand jury in session at Oklahoma City to investigate the bank's failure, Haskell issued a sharp reprimand. The grand jury was called several days before the bank failure for the purpose of investigating a breakdown in law enforcement, particularly on the prohibition front.

"I requested you to take charge of the specific investigation desired to be made," Haskell wrote West. "Affairs of the Columbia Bank & Trust Co. are under my charge for liquidation and not yet ready for full and definite consideration, and agitation at this time would be harmful to the welfare and best interests of the state."

"The governor had but one end in view, and that was to make this incident a complete triumph for the guaranty law," Robb concluded in his 1920 study. "He knew that if Norton was sent to the penitentiary the banking board would get only such part of his private fortune as could legally be taken. Haskell chose to shield Norton from prosecution and then strip him for the benefit of the depositors and the state bankers."

Norton turned over securities having a nominal value of $1,053,600. The appraised value was about $565,000, but they were in large part stocks of the most visionary oil and development enterprises which were already in the last stages of bankruptcy. What was finally realized from this personal wealth of Norton is not known.

The Columbia failure cost the other banks of the state $582,283, although the exact figure was not known until months later. Indirectly, it resulted in failure of the Farmers' National bank at Tulsa. The Tulsa bank held a $21,000 deposit for the First State bank of Kiefer which failed, as a result, on Dec. 14, 1909. With $44,000 from the guaranty fund, and quick assets of the Kiefer bank, the depositors of that bank were paid in full in eight days. The Tulsa bank, being a national institution, was not covered.

When the Bank of Ochelata closed its doors Dec. 31, 1909, Young instituted a new method of liquidating the bank through a new institution. He reported $18,968 in notes he was unable to collect. The cashier was charged with forging two notes.

"I find we can liquidate a bank much more easily through another bank located in the same town, or by permitting the failed bank to be reorganized under another name," the commissioner explained in his annual report.

Convening the second legislature in special session, Haskell told the lawmakers on Jan. 20, 1910, that individual deposits in state banks had jumped from $29,448,973 on Nov. 27, 1908, to $49,775,433 on Nov. 16, 1909—an increase of more than $20,000,000.

"Theorizing may do when we consider untried things, but two years of actual experience has qualified our people to judge of the efficiency of the Oklahoma banking law," he asserted. "It has been subjected to the severest test possible to have occurred within our state. It has arisen from this test, supreme in its power, and blessed by the people for its beneficial effects."

Oklahomans had a mania for organizing banks. Between Nov. 1, 1908, and Nov. 10, 1910, the bank commissioner reported 138 new banks. Deprived of guaranty fund membership, under the comptroller's ruling of August, 1908, 66 national banks converted to state banks while only eight state banks took out national charters.

There were 694 state banks and trust companies on Dec. 15, 1910, and E. B. Cockrell, Young's successor as commissioner, had rejected 49 charter applications since June. By comparison, Oklahoma in 1957 had 188 state and 197 national banks.

"We now have in Oklahoma about 920 national and state banks, which is an excessive number when the population of the state is taken into consideration," Cockrell wrote. He warned that too many such institutions "will be detrimental to the financial conditions in the state as a whole." The commissioner, a capable official who would continue in office several years, also made another bold suggestion to the governor:

"It has occurred to me, so long as the banking board is composed exclusively of these state officials, it will be impossible to divorce this department from politics; and to avoid the criticism which politics always engender, confidence in the official administration of this department is of supreme importance."

Haskell had demonstrated his guaranty law. The commissioner's recommendations could await a new governor.

Alarming reports of an uprising by malcontents among the Creek Indians led to the first use of the Oklahoma militia in force in March, 1909, to put down what came to be known as the "Crazy Snake rebellion." Subsequent events disclosed that Chitto Harjo, popularly dubbed "Crazy Snake," had nothing to do with the disturbance and the "rebellion" took on semi-comic aspects in the retelling after signs of danger vanished.

Harjo, whom Charles J. Barrett described as "a shrewd and forceful Indian," had come into conflict with federal authorities in 1901 by resisting the allotment of lands by the Dawes commission, then winding up its 10-year work. It was Harjo's contention that the allotment of lands to the Indians and the opening of surplus lands to white settlers constituted a breach of treaty between the United States government and the Creek nation. He and his Snake clan never agreed to the action.

Chitto Harjo—"Crazy Snake"
He was not "crazy," nor was the disturbance a "rebellion."

As the result of a disturbance at Hickory Ground, between Henryetta and Eufaula, in 1901, a troop of United States cavalry was sent from Fort Reno to take Crazy Snake into custody. He was captured, placed in the federal jail at Muskogee, and later sentenced to two years in prison for conspiring to commit treason against the federal government.

"This seemed ridiculous to persons who looked at the matter soberly," Barrett commented. Crazy Snake and nine companions were released from prison after serving a few months.

Then while Haskell was in Denver for the Democratic national convention in July, 1908, another council was held at Hickory Ground to meet Washington lobbyists employed by the Snakes. Newspapers again were filled with stories of another Snake-Creek "war." The Indians were described as being heavily armed, and threatening to fire upon white men in the neighborhood.

"And this was true, and it is also true that the Snakes could have rendered a service to the state by shooting some of these white men," Barrett observed, dryly. There was an outcry for state troops and Bellamy, as acting governor, asked Adjutant General Canton to have two companies stand ready for call. However, Canton, the old frontiersman, went in person to Hickory Ground and learned from Crazy Snake that his light horsemen bore arms to protect the camp and the women and children against lawless characters and to suppress the sale of whisky.

Crazy Snake agreed to disarm his men, but asked that he be permitted to retain their weapons, to police the camp. Canton agreed, and the excitement passed away. Crazy Snake retired to his home near Pierce, a few miles out of Eufaula, but Creek Negroes and Negroes from other states who had attended the council remained on the ground after the departure of the Snake Indians to their homes.

A village of tents and crude huts grew up. Having no means of support, the campers committed much petty thievery in the surrounding country, stealing chickens, corn and smoked meat, and occasionally killed a stray hog. Hostility developed between them and the white farmers. When local officers went to the camp on March 16, 1909, to search for stolen meat, they were fired upon and a pitched battle ensued. One Negro was killed and several white men were wounded. Most of the Negroes were arrested and placed in jail.

Suspecting Crazy Snake had been involved in the fight, a posse of deputy sheriffs was sent from Checotah to arrest him at his home. The deputies arrived about dusk, and as they emerged from the timber, they saw a number of men standing in Crazy Snake's yard. These men had been alarmed by gunfire when the deputies arrested a man in the nearby timber.

Crazy Snake's companions fled when they saw the officers, and the deputies opened fire. In the ensuing fight, two young men, Edward Baum and Herman Odom, were killed. Odom was the son of the McIntosh county sheriff. It was learned later that Crazy Snake had been shot through the calf of the leg, but he managed to escape. His home was burned to the ground, and Barrett implies the officers may have fired the house to destroy the evidence of bullet holes—made by the deputies opening fire without warning!

Urgent pleas were sent to Governor Haskell for state troops, and on March 28 Col. Roy Hoffman of Chandler with five companies of state militia was sent to the field.

Barrett, a Shawnee newspaperman who later served many years as adjutant general of the national guard and who finally attained the rank of major general, was in the expeditionary force as a major. So was Fred S. Barde, the Kansas City Star correspondent, who also held the rank of major.

A base was established at Hickory Ground, and the hills rang with bugles and the clatter of arms. The troops were prepared for active campaigning, having regular army equipment. Military telephone lines were built, and connected with rural lines.

"The country was semi-mountainous, heavily timbered, and could be traversed only with greatest difficulty," Barde recorded, "yet the unseasoned militiamen, carrying their equipment, 'hiked' 21 miles on the first day's march to Pierce, near the home of Crazy Snake, and not a man fell out of line, though many walked with painfully blistered feet . . .

"The greatest danger was in being fired upon by deputies lying in ambush in the hills . . . The constant endeavor of the troops was to capture Crazy Snake. The latter's kinsmen and friends were told to reach him if possible and tell him that Colonel Hoffman would give him the utmost protection. Crazy Snake feared that if arrested he would be placed in jail, and then mobbed by angry settlers for the death of the two deputy sheriffs."

Although the frightened Indians and Negroes took to the hills and the timber when the troops moved into camp, they soon learned the troops meant safety, and began coming from their hiding places. Scores of Indians and Negroes found scouting in the hills were arrested and taken into camp. If suspected of lawlessness, they were placed temporarily in jail. More than a hundred arrests were made, among the prisoners being Legus Jones, a son of Crazy Snake, whose English name was Wilson Jones.

Jones was pressed into service along with Thompson Tiger, an interpreter, when the troops surrounded a house near Weleetka in which they thought Crazy Snake had taken refuge. Jones and Tiger were sent forward for a parley, the latter telling Barde later:

"Here's where an Indian gets into trouble for knowing too damned much by understanding the English language and the ways of the white man." Well educated, with a good sense of humor, he spoke with a decided Celtic brogue.

"I haven't lost any Snake Indian nor anything else in this God-forsaken country. I am drawing my salary for the sole and exclusive duty of talking, not fighting, but I guess my hand has been called, so here goes."

Several frightened women and a man emerged from the house, but no Crazy Snake. It was the last night of the 10-day campaign, and the troops surrounded another house about half a mile away. This time they sent forward a woman taken from the first house.

When she failed to emerge in about five minutes, Jones and Tiger were sent to rout the inmates. Again the scared inmates, a man and half a dozen women and children, came shivering into the yard. But still no Crazy Snake, and the troops disbanded.

In 1913, Barde learned that Chitto Harjo had fled to the home of Daniel Bobs, a fullblood Choctaw living in the Kiamichi mountains near Smithville. There he died April 11, 1911, unconquered but not unsung, for Alex Posey, the great Indian poet, had dedicated a ballad to Crazy Snake. And Oklahoma's militia had had its first taste of action—$6,300 worth. At any rate, that was the amount Haskell reported to the legislature in a request for a special appropriation to defray expenses in the "Crazy Snake rebellion."

CHAPTER XII

The Capital Removal Campaign

NO incident in Oklahoma history is more befogged by legend and distortions than the removal of the capital. If the casual reader merges into one fuzzy panorama the run of 1889—which opened only six central counties—and the much larger and wilder Cherokee strip opening of 1893—stimulated by the glowing stories of the original run—there's little wonder for the confusion over the capital fight. Through two decades, hundreds of individuals played various roles in the struggle. When it reached a dramatic climax in the spectacular pre-dawn flight of W. B. Anthony with the great seal of state, it was difficult to tell which was the more surprised, Guthrie, hurt and seething over the "stolen" capital, or Oklahoma City, jubilant but unprepared for the sudden transfer.

Governor Haskell, who played the stellar role, always took a philosophical attitude toward the curious exaggerations and outright fabrications which evolved with passing years. Asked in 1932 to dictate his story of the removal, he observed, "I never spoil a good story any one wants to tell when it is in the middle, whether it is fact or just romance," and so the tall tales continued to grow.

The controversy really began May 1, 1890, with approval of the Organic act to establish territorial government. In effect, the law provided that the first legislature should meet in Guthrie, but the bill added that as soon as the legislature and governor deemed expedient, they should proceed to locate a permanent capital for Oklahoma territory.

In the first campaign, the Republicans elected a majority in both the house and council (or senate). Of the 26 house members, 14 were Republicans, nine were Democrats and three were Populists. There were seven Republicans in the council, with five Democrats and one Populist. The Republicans naturally expected to organize both houses, but they had failed to reckon with brash Oklahoma City which put capital ambitions above party. C. G. "Grist Mill" Jones and H. G.

Trosper, the Republican house members from Oklahoma county, threw in with the Democrats and Populists to elect A. N. Daniels of Canadian county, a Populist, as speaker. In the council, J. L. Brown, the Republican senator from Oklahoma county, joined the Democrats and George W. Gardenhire of Stillwater, the lone Populist, to elect Gardenhire president. In the drive to move the capital to Oklahoma City, Gardenhire was promised—and got—the Agricultural and Mechanical college for Stillwater. Edmond was promised a normal school —now Central State college—and Norman received the university.

The combination whipped through the council Council Bill No. 7 by Brown and when it came up for adoption in the house, the vote stood 14 to 12. Oklahoma City had won the capital. Then two Populist members attempted to quit the "combination," and there followed scenes of wild commotion as angry Guthrie partisans swarmed the legislative halls. Dan W. Peery, one of the Democratic members from Oklahoma county, accused of "stealing" the capital bill, was forced to flee through a back window and take refuge behind a large icebox in a meat market. Fearing for his life, Peery remained in hiding until after dark—but the incident took on humorous aspects as he related it 20 years later in a more auspicious moment.

The territorial legislature had wrangled for weeks over the capital bill, only to see the appointive governor, George W. Steele, veto the measure. Then Guthrie took prompt action to spike any more removal threats. Dennis T. Flynn, first postmaster at Guthrie, was elected as the second delegate to congress. There Flynn got inserted in the legislative appropriation bill on July 28, 1892, a provision that the legislature "shall not consider any proposition or pass any bill to remove the seat of government of said territory from its present location." Similar provisions were made in 1894, 1896 and 1898. On April 17, 1900, congress also provided that the legislature "shall not make any appropriation or enter into any contract for a capitol building." Thus congress maintained the status quo until 1906 when Bird McGuire of Pawnee, then the delegate in congress, again came to Guthrie's rescue with a proviso in the Enabling Act that the capital should remain in Guthrie until 1913.

When Henry Asp, the Republican delegate from Guthrie, offered a resolution to incorporate this provision in the constitution, Haskell arose to serve notice that he would move to table as soon as Asp had argued his proposition. Haskell said he did not believe the Enabling

Act could bind a sovereign state. If so, he asked, "haven't we accepted the Enabling Act by ordinance irrevocable?"

So the convention had, in accordance with the requirement of the act. Asp withdrew his resolution.

The question of capital location appears to have died at that point, so far as the convention was concerned; but it was a topic of conversation in the lobby of the Royal hotel and in the adjoining saloon where the "Con Con" delegates gathered to argue—over a soothing drink—prohibition, woman suffrage and other problems of the day. When Oklahoma City extended an invitation early in the convention to provide a special train and bring the delegates to a banquet, Haskell and Murray both objected, and the invitation was declined. The "Con Con" couldn't afford to interrupt sessions to be running around the state to banquets, they maintained.

In his opening remarks to the house, after election as speaker, Murray touched generally on the capital question—advocating some action to locate the capital near the geographical center of the state. His suggestion apparently was ignored, however, by both Guthrie and Oklahoma City newspapers in the excitement of the moment.

"To my notion, the legislature and the people of the state should not discriminate between any of our worthy cities, but consider the best interest of the people of the entire state," Murray asserted. "If we would but condemn or purchase a township or more of land near the center of the state, selected upon a spot having good drainage and a picturesque grandeur; lay out a town, the lots to be sold under proper business methods, the state to own the electric light plant, waterworks, street cars and all the public service institutions necessary to make a city. The sale of these lots would not only build the capitol, but would pay for all these things, together with all the institutions of the state. Look at the city of Lawton, which has accumulated from the sale of their lots more than $2,000,000. Why should not the people of Oklahoma found a city and establish a capital, not in the interests of a particular city, but in the interest of the whole people of the state, whereby they could save millions of dollars to the state, and at the same time have the most beautiful capital of any state in the American union?"

A somewhat similar proposal was advanced by Sen. Campbell Russell of Warner, who introduced a resolution for a vote on establishing a "new Jerusalem" district for the capital. Russell's measure did pass the senate, but died in the house.

On the second day of the session, Sen. P. J. Goulding of Enid offered a bill to locate the temporary capital at Enid until 1908, when he proposed the people should vote on a permanent location. Rep. I. M. Putnam of Oklahoma City introduced a resolution Feb. 11, 1908, to move legislative and administrative offices to Oklahoma City. The resolution declared the quarters in Guthrie "are in many respects inadequate and inconveniently located, and the health of many members of the legislature have been endangered by poor ventilation and insanitary conditions."

The legislature finally passed House Joint Resolution No. 11 proposing that the state acquire a site for the capital embracing ample grounds and lots to be sold for the benefit of the state. It went on the general election ballot Nov. 3, 1908, receiving 117,441 affirmative to 75,792 negative votes. While the measure failed to receive a majority of all votes cast—losing to the so-called "silent vote"—the count was an indication of public sentiment.

Meantime, the *Oklahoma State Capital* continued to snipe at Haskell and the Democratic legislature. The fight became so bitter that the *Oklahoma City Times* reported May 1, 1908, that a delegation of prominent Guthrie citizens, including Democrats and Republicans, had called on Editor Greer to counsel caution "as the town might be injured in a commercial way if the governor were driven to great anger." It was the day of red headlines—the *Capital* had installed a two-color press in 1907—and while Greer may have tempered his attacks momentarily, he was firing broadsides as Haskell waged his losing fight with Roosevelt.

Agitation to advance Oklahoma City's bid for the capital received public notice Sept. 15, 1908, when the Interstate Real Estate Exchange adopted a resolution to organize a campaign for the removal. George B. Stone, a member of the exchange and also president of the chamber of commerce, was appointed to the committee. Encouraged by the expression of sentiment at the general election, the Chamber of Commerce became active in the move in the spring of 1909. E. K. Gaylord, then business manager of *The Daily Oklahoman*, was appointed chairman of a sub-committee to outline a course of action. The second legislature was nearing the end of its session when Gaylord was called on for a report at the chamber's meeting on March 11. He said it appeared the capital bill "was dead," and he suggested a plan to initiate a petition.

"The matter was discussed by practically every member present, and finally Mr. Stone moved that Mr. Gaylord's committee be authorized to prepare a bill and initiate the same, providing for the location of the state capital in or near some incorporated city within 50 miles of the geographical center of the state," is the prosaic way the action is reported in the chamber's minutes. Four days later, at another special board meeting, Gaylord said he had just returned from conferences with the governor and Senator Russell in Guthrie. He said both were in favor of initiating a bill looking to the location of the capital "along the lines of Senator Russell's New Jerusalem plan." He detailed "the difficulties that we would have to meet" in view of the fact that Russell was in favor of a minimum of nine sections and a maximum of 16 sections on which to erect the state capitol and buildings necessary to the maintenance of all departments of the government.

On April 1, Stone brought to the meeting W. A. Ledbetter, the Ardmore attorney who had served in the constitutional convention. Ledbetter was a close friend of Haskell. Gaylord called on C. B. Ames, an outstanding lawyer, for his views, and discussion turned on three propositions. The first suggestion was a constitutional amendment, the second a proposal the capital be located on grounds within three miles of Oklahoma City, Shawnee or Guthrie. The third was a proposition advanced by Putnam, real estate promoter and member of the legislature, for a straight-out location—but within three miles of the center of the city, rather than an outlying location northwest. On April 21, Gaylord asked additional time, and on May 11 the question of financing a campaign was discussed.

Meantime, Sidney L. Brock, department store owner, had been elected to succeed Stone as chamber president, and he broke the glad news on May 18 that Oklahoma City had a chance to land a Morris & Co. packing plant. While the chamber's members turned enthusiastically to the task of wooing other packing plants, Gaylord and his committee finally presented two initiative petitions prepared by Ledbetter. One was for a proposed constitutional amendment, the other for a two-phase capital location bill.

The first was a proposition permanently to locate the capital, creating a commission of three, to be appointed by the governor, and appropriating $600,000 to purchase not to exceed 2,000 acres of land. The state would be reimbursed from the sale of lots, and a capitol

When H. G. Baker, Muskogee, resigned from Criminal Court of Appeals June 22, 1909, to organize Mid-Continent Life Insurance Co., it was occasion for unusual meeting of Governor Haskell and members of the appellate courts.

Seated, left to right: James A. "Sunny Jim" Menefee, Carnegie, state treasurer; Florence Furman, Mrs. Henry M. Furman, Governor Haskell, Mrs. Haskell, Mrs. Frank M. Canton and Thomas H. Owen, Muskogee, governor's campaign manager and Baker's successor on bench.

Second row, left to right: W. H. L. Campbell, clerk of the state supreme court; W. A. Ledbetter, legal adviser to governor; Justice Sam W. Hayes; Judge Thomas H. Doyle of the Criminal Court of Appeals; Henry M. Furman, presiding judge of criminal court; Judge Baker, Justice Robert L. Williams, Justice Jesse J. Dunn, Justice John B. Turner and Col. Berry, deputy court clerk.

Back row, left to right: W. P. "Chubby" Fields, marshal of supreme court; Reuel Haskell jr., deputy court clerk; O. T. Smith, attorney for the governor; J. A. Baker, Wewoka, a member of the "Con Con;" Charles L. Moore, assistant attorney general and member of the "Con Con;" William M. Hobbs, reporter for Judge Doyle; Adj. Gen. Frank M. Canton, Raphael Lowry, reporter for Judge Baker; Sumner Lipscomb, reporter for Judge Furman, and Jerry Esslinger, a visitor to the court.

—OKLAHOMA HISTORICAL SOCIETY PHOTOS

Above, two construction scenes at Oklahoma state penitentiary, McAlester.

—OKLAHOMA HISTORICAL SOCIETY

KATE BARNARD
She went into Kansas mines
to "rescue" state convicts.

—OKLAHOMA HISTORICAL SOCIET

JACK LOVE
He left the Santa Fe's
president standing in his office.

—FIRST CORPORATION COMMISSION REPORT

Passenger station on Missouri, Oklahoma & Gulf (now K. O. & G.) at Muskogee; Haskell built the railroad.

—OKLAHOMA HISTORICAL SOCIETY

Two street scenes from Grand, county seat of Day county; both county and town vanished from the map.

Haskell in New York, after retiring as governor.

Lee Cruce, Ardmore banker, second governor.

Bird S. McGuire, territori delegate and later congressma

—JOHN H. FREDERICKSON, JR.

When the capitol was under construction, from the contractor's progress report. Mr. Frederickson's father was superintendent of construction.

building fund thereby created. The second phase of this unusual bill submitted Guthrie, Oklahoma City and Shawnee as candidates for the voter's choice.

The proposed constitutional amendment petition received 39,-764 signatures, the location bill 27,944, and the two were presented to Leo Meyer, assistant secretary of state, on July 21, 1909. According to Meyer's sworn testimony later, Governor Haskell was present "in this very room." But for six days there was not a line in any newspaper, and the story finally broke on July 27 in the *Kansas City Journal. The Oklahoma City Times* gleefully charged that "Guthrie Sleeps on Its Rights."

Guthrie citizens, in arms, angrily charged a "conspiracy" to deprive them of the right of protest. Judge Frank Dale and other leading citizens filed a mandamus action for a hearing, alleging that the purpose in keeping the filing secret "was to prevent this plaintiff and all other persons from filing objections to said petition within five days" allowed by law.

"Plaintiff alleges that as a part of said conspiracy, it was arranged with the newspapers at Oklahoma City to publish nothing in regard to the lodging of said petition in the secretary's office, and although that fact was a news item of great interest and importance throughout the state, yet the newspapers in Oklahoma City refrained from publishing or stating anything in regard to said fact."

When Judge A. H. Huston issued the mandamus writ, Ledbetter went into the state supreme court for a writ of prohibition against the judge. He declared the initiative petition had been entered "in one of the public record books" in the office of secretary of state, and Meyer, acting for his chief, Bill Cross, who had been ill, denied there had been any attempt to conceal the fact. He said no one had asked him about the filing until O. D. Hall of the *Journal* had made inquiry.

Both Greer and Leslie G. Niblack, editor of the *Leader,* testified that their reporters had covered the secretary's office every day. Niblack admitted he had read about it in the *Times*—the story about Guthrie sleeping on its rights!

In the end, Cross held the signatures sufficient on the bill to locate the capital, and the proposed amendment petition was abandoned. On Jan. 10, 1910, Attorney General West transmitted the ballot title to the secretary of state. Then followed the presentation of arguments for and against the proposal. From Warner, Russell wrote Cross, on the stationery of the Anti-Horse Thief association, which he headed, for an opportunity to be heard.

"School is never out, 'til the big class spells," he asserted.

A. G. C. Bierer, prominent Guthrie attorney, filed the principal argument for defeat of the measure. He declared the bill would violate terms of the Enabling Act, and should be defeated; it was unconstitutional, and besides "Guthrie is centrally located, with nine railroads connecting this city with all sections of the state, and one more being built." He also pointed out that Guthrie citizens had laid out a capitol site within eight blocks of the business center and built a convention hall—at a cost of about $250,000—which they leased to the state at $1 a year. (In fact, Haskell had signed a new five-year rental contract in January.) Bierer closed by declaring: "The bill is unfair; it attempts to locate the state capital on terms dictated by one of the candidates. It permits a commission of town lot boomers to select the site for the capital and erect the capitol building."

Russell declared "the best argument against the bill is the bill itself." Paraphrasing language of the legislature, the New Jerusalem advocate wrote: "A bill by the 'peepul,' entitled an act to immediately dispose of the state capital and $600,000 in tax monies, to authorize the obligating of this state for the payment of any additional sum desired." He said it would authorize the governor to appoint three agents "who are hereby declared to be a Real Estate Corporation," and would appropriate $600,000 "to start the above authorized Real Estate Company in business . . . The said company is hereby authorized to make such location of the state capital as will best enhance the value of any real estate purchased by them, or owned by their friends, confederates or allies."

Oklahoma City replied to Guthrie's argument by declaring the bill "is fair in every particular."

"The arguments of Guthrie state that the bill initiated attempts to locate the capital on terms dictated by one candidate, and that it permits a commission of town-lot boomers to select the site for the capitol and erect the capitol building. This is a gross misstatement of facts, but it is characteristic of Guthrie's attitude upon all public matters since the Constitutional Convention was organized, and against the administration.

"The bill . . . is an appeal to the intelligence and patriotism of the voters of the state to determine whether or not they will now permanently locate the state capital, and whether it shall remain at Guthrie, the one city in this state whose every energy has been opposed to statehood and the organization and progress of state government."

On March 28, 1910, Haskell issued his proclamation for a special election June 11. As originally prepared, the proclamation set the date for Tuesday, June 14, but with his pen the governor marked out "fourteenth" and substituted "eleventh"—a Saturday. That meant the

no appeal has been taken from the action of the Secretary of State in approving the sufficiency of said petition or in relation thereto.

NOW THEREFORE, I, Charles N. Haskell, Governor of the State of Oklahoma, by virtue of the authority vested in me by the Constitution and laws of the State of Oklahoma, do hereby proclaim and make known that the date of the referendum vote on said measure will be on the ~~fourteenth (14th)~~ Eleventh (11) day of June in the year of our Lord One Thousand Nine Hundred and Ten, and I do hereby further proclaim and call a special election to be held throughout the State of Oklahoma on the said date for the [illegible] purpose of such referendum vote.

~~[illegible]~~

IN TESTIMONY WHEREOF I have hereunto set my hand, and caused the great seal of the State of Oklahoma to be hereto affixed this 28th day of March in the year of our Lord One Thousand Nine Hundred and Ten, and of the Independence of the United States of America, the one hundred and thirty-fourth.

C N Haskell

GOVERNOR.

Closing portion of Haskell's proclamation for special election on removal of capital. Note that governor changed date from Tuesday to Saturday. Did he contemplate a repetition of Sunday coup in building railroad through Ottawa?

results would become known on Sunday. Was the former railroad promoter mindful of another Sunday, years earlier, when he laid the tracks through Ottawa, Ohio, on the sabbath and thus avoided court injunctions? He also submitted for the same date a proposed amendment to Section 9, Article IX, under which transportation companies might buy parallel and competing lines.

Guthrie was in a dilemma. Her leading attorneys argued the bill ran counter to the Enabling Act; should she fight through the courts, or at the polls? Editor Niblack raised the question at a mass meeting March 31, and a legal committee, including Dale and Bierer, was appointed.

TEMPORARY CAPITAL BUILDING

Built by Citixens of Guthrie at a Cost of $200,00.00
and used by the State

Whr Spend MIllions for a Capital Location at This Time?

VOTE AGAINST THE BILL JUNE 11TH AND KEEP DOWN YOUR TAXES

Taxpayers, citizens, sovereigns of Oklahoma, do you realize that you are face to face with a question involving the honor of the state, the integrity of its citizenship, the stability of every institution, and the right of yourselves and your children after you?

The state capital location bill inaugurated and fostered by the real estate speculators of Oklahoma City for selfish personal gain, is one of the most iniquitous schemes ever attempted in the name of legislation. Under the guise of a general law for locating the state capital it seeks to [illegible]

itol and other institutions. They are further authorized TO SPEND ALL OF THE MONEY THEY RECEIVE from the sale of lots, for salaries, improvements and other expenses.

The fact that the commissioners are [illegible]thorized to reserve part of the land "for other institutions" shows the evident [illegible]tent of the men back of the [illegible] many of the state [illegible] this location.

These three men are [illegible]

A sample of Guthrie's futile campaign to retain capital.

At the next meeting, Bierer reported there was no way to enjoin the election; "the only thing to do is win it at the polls." Judge Dale, presiding at a meeting April 16, declared: "We are in this fight to stick, and stick successfully. If we fight as we ought to fight we will win it. If we don't, we won't. First, we should let the people of this state know why the capital should not be removed. It should be borne home to their upright consciousness that it is unfair, dishonest and expensive. They should be told that we have built a $200,000 convention hall and set it in the midst of 10 as pretty acres as there are in Oklahoma, without one penny of expense to the state."

Niblack, who had married Haskell's daughter, Frances, on March 31, 1909, revealed some insight in the governor's feelings toward Guthrie.

"The governor doesn't like Guthrie, and doesn't mince words in saying so. That's personal," he wrote in the *Leader*, March 30, 1910.

"In a measure, the governor has some valid ground for personal dislike of Guthrie by personal actions of certain citizens two or three years ago, and by the constant abuse of the Republican (*Capital*) daily paper here . . . Guthrie, as a city, was not responsible because drunken hoodlums in the Elks club mutilated a picture of the governor; nor was Guthrie as a city responsible because former Governor Frantz of Enid acted the jackass and refused to participate in the first state inaugural ceremonies . . . As a city, Guthrie has made mistakes, but tries to do the right thing."

On the other hand, Oklahoma City took the initiative. Enthusiastic city boosters carried the story of the growing metropolis—the population* had nearly doubled in three years, from 32,452 in 1907 to 64,205 in 1910—on their annual trade tour through the state. In its efforts to raise campaign money, Oklahoma City sponsored "tag day" on Saturday, May 28, with $3,303.42 in net receipts. The baseball club donated 90 percent of game receipts for three days, the theaters chipped in

*Some comparative census statistics between 1907 and 1910 reflect the growth of the larger cities:

	1907	1910		1907	1910
Enid	10,087	13,799	Oklahoma City	32,452	64,205
Guthrie	11,652	11,654	Sapulpa	4,259	8,283
Lawton	5,562	7,788	Shawnee	10,955	12,474
Muskogee	14,418	25,278	Tulsa	7,298	18,182

The total population of the new state increased from 1,414,177 in 1907 to 1,657,155 in 1910.

amounts ranging from 25 to 50 percent of ticket sales, and the Oklahoma City Bar association called on the courts to adjourn from June 1 through June 13 to permit the lawyers to lend "their patriotic efforts to secure the capital of Oklahoma for Oklahoma City."

Party lines disappeared in the common cause. George H. Dodson, the Republican county chairman, and Sam A. Calhoun, the Democratic chairman, called a joint meeting of their committees for June 4 to unite forces. O. B. Kee was designated to recruit citizens to return to their former home towns and line up votes.

Charles F. Colcord, early-day marshal who had made a fortune in the Glenn pool, headed the campaign organization, but every one had a hand in activities. W. L. Alexander, Democratic wheelhorse, headed the speakers' bureau. Dennis Flynn, the early-day delegate to congress, had established law offices in Oklahoma City, and with C. G. Jones and other Republican stalwarts, he entered the fray.

New booster trains were organized and, loaded with enthusiasts, left Sunday midnight, June 5, to canvass the state. F. A. Wharten, a representative of the Pioneer Telephone Co., aboard one train, would install a long distance telephone at night so that the Oklahoma City men could call home free of charge. One sour note from the booster trips, heard months later, led indirectly to incorporation of the Oklahoma City chamber of commerce. That resulted from a claim for expenses by Dorset Carter, Purcell, president of the Oklahoma Central railroad. It came to light in October when Carter, who had advanced $2,697 for the booster trains, complained that the boosters had neglected to plug for the amendment to Article IX. Carter was counting on this amendment to help him unload the 128-mile Central railroad, connecting Lehigh and Chickasha, on one of the interstate lines. When the amendment failed, Carter asked for his money back. The chamber finally offered to compromise by returning $1,000. When it was pointed out that each member might be held personally liable "just as a partnership . . . for the entire amount of any debts against the chamber of commerce," the board on October 25 appointed a committee to draw up articles of incorporation.

CHAPTER XIII

Haskell's Story of the Removal

CAME the big day, June 11, and 160,000 Oklahomans flocked to the polls—men only. Activity centered in Oklahoma City, Guthrie and Shawnee, where teams were organized to get the voters out. Twenty-two years later Haskell dictated for the author his story of the occasion:

"Mrs. Haskell and I came home (to Muskogee) on the tenth of June so as to be at home and vote on the eleventh. During the day of the eleventh, we were invited by the Commercial club of Tulsa to attend a banquet the club was giving the night of the eleventh.

"We reached Tulsa during the day and were there from perhaps 4 o'clock in the afternoon until after midnight, attending this banquet. Of course, by the close of the eleventh, the battle of ballots was over, and at Tulsa we were at Tate Brady's hotel. Before going to the banquet, I asked Brady to get on the telephone and while we were gone to the banquet, to gather all the votes on the capital question possible.

"We returned just about midnight to the Brady hotel, and Brady had been wonderfully effective in getting election returns. He had a list of a vast majority of the precincts of the state which showed 98,-000 plus (sic) for Oklahoma City, 24,000 plus for Guthrie and 7,000 plus for Shawnee. It was almost a complete precinct return.

"I at once said to Brady, 'When can we get a train to Oklahoma City?' He said, 'Not until tomorrow, as the midnight train has already gone.' Then I told him: 'Call the division office of the Frisco railroad on the telephone.' I think it was then at Sapulpa. In a very few minutes I had the superintendent's office on the telephone and asked him to send a locomotive and a coach to Tulsa at once to make an Oklahoma City trip. In about 30 or 40 minutes, the special engine and a sleeping car were ready for us.

"I looked about and invited every Oklahoman in sight to make the trip, and a number went with us straight to Oklahoma City. That number included some who (in 1932) are still living: Bob Galbreath and his wife, Tate Brady and his wife, and several others. We all took this special train and went directly to Oklahoma City, reaching the Lee hotel about 6 o'clock the morning of the 12th.

"The last thing before leaving Tulsa, I had telephoned my then private secretary, W. B. Anthony, at Guthrie to get the secretary of state with his official seal and meet us at the Lee-Huckins hotel in Oklahoma City, early in the morning. When we walked into the hotel, the whole crowd of us, at 6 o'clock in the morning of the twelfth, Bill Cross, secretary of state, and Anthony were there waiting for us.

"We really had been visiting all night, and had not been asleep, and everybody was hungry. They found a place for breakfast and somebody said, 'Well, let's go in and get our breakfast.' I said, 'just wait a minute.' I stepped up to the clerk's desk in the hotel, got a sheet of paper—the hotel letterhead—a pen and ink and wrote the official proclamation based on the returns which I thought were plainly adequate, declaring 'Oklahoma City the capital of the State of Oklahoma.'

"I signed it as governor, Bill Cross put his official signature and seal on this proclamation and, complying with the law which said such proclamations should be posted in a public place, I posted it on the wall of the Lee hotel adjoining the clerk's desk.

"Then I said, 'Very well, now I am ready to have breakfast in the state capital.' "

Anthony related his role in bringing the seal of state from Guthrie in an interview with Joe O'Brien, a veteran statehouse reporter, on June 19, 1927. Taking note of the growing myths, O'Brien declared "the name of Anthony, the real and only principal in the seal removal, has almost been lost entirely in the mesh of bogus claims, exaggerations and misinformation emanating from would-be authoritative spokesmen of the history-making flight."

Anthony, a Marlow newspaperman who had served in the first legislature, told O'Brien he had been home to vote and was in Oklahoma City on his way back to Guthrie when he received Haskell's call from Tulsa. He gave O'Brien this account:

"I had been to Marlow to vote and had returned to Oklahoma City on my way back to Guthrie. About midnight Governor Haskell called me and told me to proceed to the office of the secretary of state at Guthrie, and get the seal of state and the book in which the secretary records executive acts, and bring them immediately to Oklahoma City.

"Feeling at Guthrie at the time was quite intense, and I did not believe it the proper thing to do to go on the train, so I decided to make the trip in an automobile. The car was furnished by the chamber of commerce of Oklahoma City. I do not recall the name of the driver. It was a rented car. The driver's brother at the time, I think, was superintendent of the water works in Oklahoma City. 'Gov.' S. F. Price came around about that time and asked permission to go along.

"In the meantime, Bill Cross, secretary of state, had communicated with Earl Keys who was, at the time, an employee at the office, and told him to meet me at my room in Henry Wilmering's home at Guthrie and do what I would tell him to do. I also called (Paul) Nesbitt, who was chief clerk in the governor's office, and went directly to my room, arriving there about 3 o'clock in the morning. I told them of Governor Haskell's instructions and directed them to proceed accordingly. I had left a bundle of laundry in the governor's office, and a few articles of clothing. Keys, Nesbitt and (Porter) Spaulding (an employee in the governor's office) entered the building, telling the guards they were after my laundry.

"The seal of state and the recording book were concealed in the bundle of laundry and clothing and removed from the building to my room without any one except the principals ever knowing what was going on. I never went to the office for to have done so might have aroused suspicion.

"After the seal and book had been turned to me, I leisurely prepared for the return trip to Oklahoma City. We left Guthrie about 4 o'clock and arrived in Oklahoma City at 7 o'clock on Sunday morning, June 12, in what was altogether a very uneventful trip, as compared with what has since been said of it."

Anthony was destined to play a more eventful role in the final act of removing the capital and building a statehouse, but Keys—for many years thereafter an office supply salesman at the capitol—added his version in 1952. Provoked by a newspaper picture of a recessed and shadowed window in the Logan county courthouse through which, the newspaper story claimed, "a man carrying the great seal clambered, on the evening of June 11, a car waiting for him in the alley, then rushed to Oklahoma City and Oklahoma City had a capital," Keys declared: "The only part of that story which is true is the picture of the window."

His version of the seal removal was vouched for also by Luther Harrison, for more than 30 years chief editorial writer for *The Daily Oklahoman.* Harrison, at the time press secretary in Democratic state headquarters, was loafing around the Lee-Huckins hotel when Anthony embarked on his night ride, and went along for the ride without knowing the mission. He was so modest about his role that years later he did a short news story about the "ignorant young man" who didn't learn till the next day the real object of the trip.

Keys said he received a long distance call from Cross about 7 p. m. advising that Anthony would be in Guthrie about 11 p. m. "with a message for me from him and told me to do what the message requested.

"That night about 11 o'clock, Secretary Cross telephoned again, and said that there had been a slight delay in the time when Anthony would arrive but that when he did arrive in Guthrie, he would telephone me at my residence . . . Early Sunday morning, at daylight, the telephone rang and when I went to the telephone, Anthony was on the line. He said, 'Earl, this is Bill Anthony. Can you come down to your office?' I dressed, walked down to the courthouse on East Harrison avenue and in front of the courthouse I saw a Cadillac touring car.

"When I arrived at the north entrance of the courthouse and looked at the car and its passengers, I saw the driver, Bill Light, and Anthony in the front seat; in the rear seat were Porter Spaulding, an employee of the governor's office, 'Gov.' S. F. Price, an old friend of Secretary Cross, and Luther Harrison . . . at that time press agent for the Democratic state central committee, and who, by the way, had invited himself and went along for the ride without any idea of where they were going or knowing the purpose of the mission. While the car left Oklahoma City at 11 o'clock that night, it was daylight when it arrived at Guthrie due to a flat tire near Seward, on unpaved highways and poor country roads.

"When I stepped over to the car, Anthony said, 'Earl, let's go into your office.' He and I walked up the steps of the courthouse and were met at the door by Night Watchman Dooley Williamson who opened the door and said, 'Earl, what do you want?' I told him I had some business in the office and he spoke to Anthony, and Anthony and I walked down the hall and unlocked the door.

"Anthony handed me a written note from Secretary Cross telling me to deliver the great seal of the State of Oklahoma, of which the secretary of state has always been the custodian, to Anthony. The seal was kept in an iron safe in the vault, along with the Constitution. I went to the vault and opened the safe and lifted the seal out and went into the room and wrote out a receipt on the typewriter. Anthony signed it, and I wrapped the seal in a piece of brown kraft wrapping paper. Anthony put it under his arm and we walked down the hall and out of the building. He got in the car and drove straight to Oklahoma City, where he delivered the great seal to Secretary Cross and it has remained in Oklahoma City ever since.

"Temporary offices of the governor and secretary of state were set up immediately on the second floor of the Lee-Huckins hotel, and a proclamation declaring Oklahoma City the victor in the election was issued by Governor Haskell and the impression of the seal placed thereon. From then on, and until the removal of the capitol records from Guthrie, and during the court and all legal proceedings which followed this election, the seal remained in Oklahoma City and was used on all state documents requiring its use. . . . I regret that I did not keep the letter from Secretary Cross or the receipt which I had Anthony sign for the seal, but at that time I did not think of its historical value. Whatever became of the piece of kraft wrapping paper which covered the seal when Anthony left the office is, to my mind, the only mysterious part of the removal of the seal from Guthrie, and the true story of the removal is exactly as I have related it."

Fred P. Branson of Muskogee, later chief justice of the state supreme court, had been elected Democratic state chairman on May 19, 1910, and had headquarters at the Lee-Huckins. He said the special train had been financed by Robert Galbraith, one of the discoverers of the Glenn pool, Tate Brady and John O. Mitchell, mayor of Tulsa. Writing in the *Oklahoma Chronicles* in 1953, Branson said the train arrived about 7:30 a. m. and word having been sent ahead, a group including Colcord, Ledbetter, C. G. Jones, Edgar S. Vaught and Dennis Flynn was on hand to greet the governor.

"When Governor Haskell was located in his hotel suite surrounded as he was by these men, his first exclamation was, 'Get me a stenographer!' The Hon. Dennis Flynn, who was never known to fail to meet an emergency, in double quick time secured a stenographer and the governor then and there and in the presence of those assembled dictated a proclamation declaring Oklahoma City to be capital of the State of Oklahoma," Branson related. News of Haskell's action spread rapidly and by noon *The Oklahoman* had an extra on the streets.

Before the polls had closed on Saturday, however, Guthrie citizens had rushed into district court for an injunction to prevent removal of capitol offices. Still whistling in the dark, the *Capital* reported scattered returns from the election under a two-line banner:

Complete Election Returns Show Death Of The Location Bill

About the only support the *Capital* found for its headlines was in the Guthrie returns: On the location proposition, 2,707 no, 54 yes; on the capital site selection, Guthrie, 2,632; Oklahoma City, 30, and Shawnee, 5. A bold-faced line set the mood for returns from out in the state: *Mangum Votes Wrong*. The count showed Oklahoma City, 501; Guthrie, 32, and Shawnee 6.

The *Capital* had no Monday edition, but on Tuesday, June 14, Editor Greer pulled all stops in his attack on Haskell. Red headlines proclaimed: *"Czar Charles Issues his Imperial Ukase at New State 'Capital.'"*

If state officials were in a quandary, Oklahoma City was stunned. Sidney L. Brock, president of the chamber of commerce, issued a statement approved at a special meeting on Monday. It read:

"Oklahoma City's chamber of commerce, business men and citizens in general were greatly surprised at the sudden call by Governor Haskell for state quarters, and by the announcement that the seat of government is now transferred to Oklahoma City. We had no intimation or thought that the capital would be removed until 1913, and were quite sincere in our campaign statements that there would be no effort by the chamber of commerce or citizens of Oklahoma City to remove the state capital before 1913."

That had been the position of Oklahoma City boosters in the campaign. The *Times* had commented editorially on May 5, "there has been objection to the removal of the capital prior to 1913 on the ground that Oklahoma accepted the Enabling Act. The bill does provide for the location of the permanent capital and provides for the construction of the capitol building. It would be impossible to complete a capitol building prior to 1913," and again on May 12 the *Times* observed: "Oklahoma City . . . does not propose to bring the state capital to Oklahoma City before 1913. The vote at this time is to fix the town where the capital shall be located permanently."

In a front page editorial on June 14, *The Oklahoman* said:

"In the contest for the location of the permanent seat of state government of Oklahoma, just closed, *The Oklahoman* represented, and the people of Oklahoma City represented, that this city was content to let the seat of government remain at Guthrie until 1913, as provided by the Enabling Act.

"The action of Governor Haskell, therefore, in proclaiming Oklahoma City the capital of the state and recognizing it as the capital comes as a distinct surprise to us . . . *The Oklahoman* rather regrets that this situation has arisen. It cannot help but feel that our word was out to the people of the state in this matter, and it has no other desire than to keep faith with them. And, speaking for the people of this city, we are confident that we voice the uniform sentiment in saying that we do not want the capital before 1913 . . . With Governor Haskell, the case, of course, is different. As the governor of the state, it becomes his bounden duty to observe the law. The only law we have relating to the capital location was enacted by the people last Saturday.

"So we trust the people of the state will appreciate the rather embarrassing situation thrust upon us by the governor's action. We want them to understand that Oklahoma City has had no hand in this immediate removal of the capital . . ."

The state supreme court and most state officers chose to remain in Guthrie, in view of the temporary injunction issued by Judge Huston. From Guthrie came reports that Sheriff John Mahoney had stationed 50 armed guards around the courthouse. When Charles L. Dougherty, state labor commissioner, was halted leaving the building, there were bitter words. When two deputies attempted to serve Haskell with a summons, he brushed them aside, but on Sunday night he dictated a letter to J. H. Burford, one of the attorneys who obtained the injunction:

"This advises you as attorney representing the citizens of Guthrie that upon consideration of the law and the facts and the public health, peace and welfare, that I find and consider the capital of the state of Oklahoma to be at Oklahoma City, state of Oklahoma, by virtue of the law adopted and enacted by an overwhelming majority of the people of the sovereign state of Oklahoma on June 11, 1910, and that the official business of the state cannot lawfully be conducted except at the state capital.

"It comes to my notice that many of the people of Oklahoma City, as well as your clients, have construed said law as permitting said state capital to remain at Guthrie until some future date.

"This is to advise you that in case you desire a hearing before me on this question, I shall grant you such hearing at 2 p. m. June 14, 1910, at the office in the Lee-Huckins hotel in Oklahoma City, whereat any rights you may have will be fully considered. I accord you this, not desiring to do your clients any injustice, nor to have the interest of the state in any way hindered or embarrassed by your resorting to injunctions or any other technical, legal warfare, expensive and annoying to the public welfare."

Guthrie ignored the invitation, of course. In a newspaper interview, Haskell reiterated his views: "While some newspapers have stated that the capital was to remain in Guthrie until 1913, under the bill, it is my business to construe this law, and I said in a speech 10 days ago that nobody was construing this law for the governor. I said then that if the bill passed, the capital would legally be placed at Oklahoma City —and that immediately."

In commenting on Brock's apology for the Oklahoma City chamber of commerce on the governor's hasty action, *The Capital* declared: "Their plot to steal the state capital was born in iniquity and their every movement has been that of skulking law breakers and libertines."

Haskell gave an insight into his fast action in moving the capital when he spoke at a victory celebration at the fair grounds on the Wednesday following. *The Oklahoman* reported about 15,000 enthusiastic citizens in attendance, while other thousands lined the parade line from the hotel. The governor and Mrs. Haskell, with Mayor and Mrs. Henry M. Scales, led the procession in Jack Jones' new $5,000 Oldsmobile, with squads of mounted policemen on either side. It was the "longest and most successful automobile parade ever given in Oklahoma City," the paper added.

"It has never been the policy of the present governor of Oklahoma to let another man get to first base before he gets there himself," Haskell told the cheering crowd. "If there are to be any injunction suits, he proposes to let those suits find him where he wants to be, rather than at the place from which he is trying to get from, and that is why the official seat of government for the state of Oklahoma today is in Oklahoma City.

"I have but one regret in this matter, and that is that Bill Cross beat me to the new capital city, and I was not slow in getting here, either. Bill came 24 hours ahead of me to vote and (turning to Secretary of State Cross), how many times did you vote, Bill? When I got here at 6 o'clock, Bill was eating breakfast in what he then termed the 'new statehouse.'

"I am glad to know, however, that Oklahoma City and its men who have made this vigorous campaign for the state capital, hesitate to accept the capital at this time, if they think they have gained it by deception. Your chamber of commerce, however, may rest in peace, for you haven't stolen anything!

"When I noticed before the election that Oklahoma City said that it didn't want the capital before 1913, I in my address stated that the law would take its course, and that your conception that the capital should not be moved before 1913 was wrong. I knew that the law would make immediate removal necessary, for the constitution says that the business of the state must be transacted at the state capital . . . I claim nothing for the part which I took in this capital fight; I merely took the part of the people of the state, and since I came to Oklahoma City, it is the first time in almost three years that my wife has quit wishing for my term of office to stop."

The next day, Haskell issued the proclamation now on file with the secretary of state. It set forth the official count: for Oklahoma City, 96,261; for Guthrie 31,301, and for Shawnee, 8,382.

Guthrie's fight soon reached the state supreme court, but meantime on August 23 Haskell appointed the capitol commission called for under the initiative petition and on the same day the commission entered into agreement on the so-called Putnam site. Haskell's close friend, Tate Brady of Tulsa, was selected as chairman. J. B. A. Robertson of Chandler, former district judge, was the other Democratic member and Dr. Leo Bennett of Muskogee—whose wife had been the "bride" representing Indian territory at the inaugural—was named the Republican member.

I. M. Putnam, a representative in both the first and second legislatures and a venturesome real estate promoter, and John W. Shartel, general manager of the Oklahoma Railway Co., were the prime movers in a plan to offer the state 1,600 acres and $1,700,000 in cash. The site was northwest of Oklahoma City on the El Reno interurban line in what came to be known as Putnam City. The $1,700,000 would include $1,500,000 for a capitol, $150,000 for furniture and equipment, $40,000 for salaries and expenses of the commission and $10,000 for moving offices from Guthrie.

"I am convinced that the 1,600 acres of land is certain to produce the funds mentioned," Haskell said, in announcing the agreement, "and that these public-spirited citizens who have donated their land for this purpose will * * * have returned to them any surplus of said land after the state has received its full amount of money required for the above purposes." The commission took options until December 20.

On November 15, the supreme court knocked out the initiative petition. In an opinion by Justice Turner in the suit prosecuted by James Hepburn, the Logan county County Attorney, against Thomas P. Smith, then secretary of state, the court held unanimously that the petition had a fatal error through omission of the question "shall it be adopted."

"We are therefore of the opinion that the statute has not been complied with," the court declared. The opinion came down a week after the general election, in which Lee Cruce of Ardmore won the governorship and the voters chose members of the third legislature. Terms of the old house members and half the senate would expire 15 days after the election. When advised of the ruling, Haskell commented: "One question . . . is conclusively settled, and that is that the people of Oklahoma had the right to select their own capital at any time after we became a state." He deferred speculation on his next move, but informed the newspapers:

"When I have arrived at a conclusion that I believe is sound, I shall announce it to the people of Oklahoma, and where action is necessary, that action will be open and vigorous."

Haskell's first grandchild, Lillian Elizabeth, was born to the Leslie Niblacks on October 26. Dropping the hint that he was going to see his granddaughter, Haskell entered a "fast automobile" on Saturday, November 19, and headed for Guthrie. After a leisurely lunch with his daughter and son-in-law, the governor strolled down to the courthouse and signed a proclamation convening the new legislature in special session at Oklahoma City for November 28 to locate the capital. He could under the constitution convoke the legislature at any place he deemed proper "for the public peace and safety," although the action would have to be ratified later by two-thirds vote of the legislature.

"I told these Guthrie people a year ago," he informed the assembled newsmen, "that if they didn't see that Frank Greer quit calling me a liar every morning, I would get into this capital fight." In an accompanying statement, he asserted that "every principle contended for on behalf of the people has been sustained by the court. The only defeat was in the technical language and expression of the measure voted on by the people."

The granddaughter is now Mrs. George Melton of Tulsa.

When the legislature met at the Lee-Huckins on the appointed day, Haskell's former secretary, W. B. Anthony, was chosen speaker of the house and J. Elmer Thomas of Lawton was elected president pro tempore of the senate. The house promptly ratified the governor's call, 80 to 26, and the senate gave its approval, 33 to 9. In his message to the joint session, Haskell recounted the efforts to move the capital from Guthrie since the first territorial legislature in 1890, adding:

"By a direct vote of the people, or through their representatives elected to the legislature, the question of changing the capital city has five times been voted and every time the vote has carried to change the capital. I call your attention to the fact that Guthrie has no claim, legal, equitable or moral, to the honor of being the capital city. It has at all times sought to defeat the will of the people by an appointive governor's veto, by court litigation or by acts of congress unwarranted and unauthorized; Guthrie has at all times received substantial payment from the people for every favor the territory or state has had. Our taxpayers are even yet today paying substantially $23,000 per year for the rent and maintenance of offices in Guthrie . . . The entire expense of this special session need not equal more than six months' office rent now being paid at the present capital . . .

"Gentlemen of the legislature, I have completed the duty devolving upon me and it rests with you solely and in your own judgment to give the people in substance and effect the law that they clearly intended to adopt."

As an afterthought, Haskell sent a special message recommending the legislature confer original jurisdiction on the supreme court in any litigation arising from the capital removal. Bills were introduced promptly to establish a permanent seat of government in Oklahoma City, but the one destined for final adoption was house bill No. 7—the same number as that on the original council bill in 1890 and on the initiative petition—by Reps. J. H. Wright of Oklahoma City, Dan W. Peery of Carnegie and W. A. Durant of Durant.

Although the house appeared willing to go along on the Putnam site, opposition soon developed in the senate. Charles F. Colcord, C. G.

Jones, Edgar S. Vaught and other citizens who had played an active role in the June campaign came forward with plans for a location nearer the heart of the city on Northeast Twenty-second street at its juncture with a half-section line known as Lincoln boulevard. W. F. Harn, owning land west of Lincoln boulevard, which he had staked in the run of 1889, and J. J. Culbertson, real estate developer with land on the east, joined forces to swing the location to the east-side location. The senate appointed a capitol location committee headed by J. B. Thompson of Pauls Valley.

While an informal agreement appears to have been reached December 11, the *Times* reported a mass meeting in the Levy building (now the Mercantile, at Main and Hudson) on the twelfth. With Vaught presiding, 25 business men signed bonds for $5,000 each as a guarantee that Oklahoma City would give the state free a $1,000,000 capitol.

"The plot of ground on which the capitol is proposed to be built is high and level and commands an excellent view of the city," reported the *Times*. "It will be about a seven-minute ride from the downtown section by trolley with an excellent service guaranteed by the two double track systems."

The next day Thompson's committee quashed the Putnam site with a report charging the agreement was void anyway.

"Our investigation disclosed that said Putnam site is from seven to nine miles by the usual method of travel from the center of Oklahoma City, and that the best and quickest time hoped for from rapid transit service is a 20-minute schedule each way . . . We further report that the said proposed site is north of the present packing plant . . . and in the path of the prevailing winds of this section . . . We further suggest that said Putnam site is not backed by Oklahoma City, and only urged by persons interested in that particular section of the city . . . and, further, if said site had been definitely proposed and guaranteed, in our opinion, it would not be a desirable site for the location of the permanent seat of government."

Despite a vigorous fight by Sen. Reuben M. Roddie of Ada, the report carried, 35 to 4, with four excused. Sen. Thomas F. McMechan of Oklahoma City, owning property near the eastside site, declared a personal interest and refrained from voting.

Now Colcord, Vaught and 29 others—including Mrs. McMechan, the only woman signer—reduced their agreement to writing and posted bond for $100,000 for performance. They proposed to organize the State Capitol Building Co. "for the purpose of acting as trustee in behalf of said persons above mentioned and their associates, as donors." The agreement called for 15 acres for the capitol site—astraddle Lincoln boulevard—to be given free.

The building company would secure title to 650 acres, to be conveyed to the state, "the proceeds from the sale of said lands . . . to be held in trust for the state." Legal title to the property would remain in the company "but proceeds from the sale of said lands, after paying the expenses herein provided for, shall be a trust fund in the hands of said company for the benefit of the state . . . until said company shall have paid, as provided in the proposal to the State of Oklahoma, the said sum of $1,000,000."

The amended bill was whipped through both houses the next day, December 16, and Speaker Anthony appointed Dan Peery to accompany a senate committee in taking the bill to the governor. By a quirk of fate, it had been 20 years since the youthful Peery, as a representative from Oklahoma county, had fled a Guthrie mob infuriated over the first bill to remove the capital.

Dan W. Peery

It took him exactly 20 years to deliver capital bill to governor.

During a lull in proceedings, he told the story of that 1890 incident to an attentive house. He recounted the "Combination's" successful efforts to get the bill through the Council and the house, and his dismay to return from the telegraph office to learn that Populist members had r e n e g e d. "T h r o u g h some subtle influence, known only to Guthrie financiers, two Populist members of our combination had deserted us." They had moved to reconsider the motion to reconsider, the tabling of which is the customary parliamentary procedure for nailing down passage of a bill.

"It was the most unparliamentary thing imaginable," Peery added. During the noon recess, the Oklahoma City partisans decided to pull a coup. Since the bill had cleared both houses, and Peery was on the joint committee on enrolled and engrossed bills, he decided to have the bill enrolled and signed by the presiding officers. Peery got Speaker A. N. Daniels to sign the bill in the house, and took it to the council, only to find that body had adjourned. He handed the bill to R. J. Nesbitt, of Cleveland county, and went out on the street to find a mass of people "from the opera house clear up to the corner."

"The first thing I noticed, the crowd had hold of Daniels, the speaker. Daniels cried, 'Peery has the bill,' and the crowd came after me, and then I ran. And don't you know, the whole city of Guthrie came after me at that time! They gathered around in scores and were crying for a rope and made all manner of demonstrations, declaring I had stolen the capital bill." Peery took refuge in a butcher shop.

The butcher was out—"in the chase, I suppose"—when Peery hid behind the icebox. When the butcher returned in midafternoon, he was accompanied by another man, and Peery said he heard the second man say: "If they get that man Peery, they will hang him," and . . . the butcher said, "Damn him, they ought to hang him; he has stolen the capital bill!"

Peery remained in hiding until after dark, when he slipped out and hid in "Grist Mill" Jones' room. When the Oklahoma City crowd gathered at dinner that night, they agreed that should the bill be vetoed, they would support Kingfisher for the capital.

"In five days after its passage," Peery continued, "the 'Carpetbag' governor, George W. Steele from Marion, Ind., vetoed the bill. Before that long and eventful session closed, we voted the capital of Oklahoma to Kingfisher twice. I shall not attempt to give a history of the proceedings on the Kingfisher bills. But Guthrie has had the capital ever since; but she won't have it when this session adjourns."

Final approval of the capital bill was delayed an hour in the senate when Senator Thompson declared it was the sentiment of the capitol location committee that the Oklahoma City chamber of commerce should be required to give written guarantee of free quarters for state departments pending construction of the capitol building. Sen. Frank M. Colville of Britton hurried off to confer with Brock and S. C. Heyman, returning with assurances such free quarters "positively will be provided."

The legislature then adjourned, on December 16, but Oklahoma City was due another jolt. Haskell let it be known that the city would have to raise $71,200 to wind up the Putnam deal before he would sign the capital bill. The request included $9,200 for Putnam, $30,000 for architect fees, $14,000 for attorneys representing Oklahoma City in the capital fight, and $18,000 for expenses of the old capitol commission and interest on $70,000 advanced by the state to build temporary quarters. Although dismayed, Brock called in leading business men and they set to work.

By 6:30 p. m. on December 29, the citizens committee reported to the governor that it had raised $66,000, and to make good on the remainder, the members had organized a capitol expense company. The governor accepted their pledge and boarded a 7:10 p. m. train for Guthrie accompanied by Ledbetter.

The northbound Santa Fe would meet a southbound train at Guthrie. Haskell and Ledbetter disembarked at Guthrie, went into the Harvey house for a cup of coffee, and there at 8:40 p. m. he signed the three bills which finally moved the capital. The last official act in Guthrie was the governor's signature taking the capital away.

As the train bearing Governor Haskell reached Oklahoma City at 10:20 p. m., "whistles screeched, bells rang and auto horns tooted," the *Times* reported. The governor was met by a reception committee and paraded to the Lee-Huckins hotel. After 20 years of struggle, Oklahoma City was definitely and finally the capital of Oklahoma.

CHAPTER XIV

The Four-Ring Circus Debates

WHILE the capital removal fight overshadowed the campaign for governor in the early weeks, the candidates had not been idle. Lee Cruce, the Ardmore banker, announced for a second try in November, 1909. Loser to Haskell by some 3,000 votes in the pre-statehood primary, Cruce had been honored with appointment to the University board of regents, while his brother, A. C. Cruce, had been one of the principal attorneys defending Haskell in the lot fraud cases.

Murray, exhausted by the strenuous work of the Constitutional Convention and the first legislature, spent months regaining his health on his farm near Tishomingo. Choosing Altus for his opening speech —largely because he claimed credit for "fathering" Jackson county in the "Con Con"—Murray announced on April 19. Then occurred a small incident which was to assume big proportions in the campaign; and it illustrates, too, the influence of Civil war passions half a century later.

Streets were lined with people, and Murray was assigned to ride in a buggy with a pretty girl to the public square. Looking down the line of parade, he noted some Confederate veterans with a Confederate flag, but no U. S. flag in the line of march. When he asked the girl about the flag, she said: "In our hurry, we left it in the yard."

"It dawned on me immediately that even nominated, I might have a hard contest in the north part of the state with northern Democrats, and it might cause my defeat," he wrote in his Memoirs. "Moreover, I was born four years after the war was over and so far as I was concerned, the war was over, and it was 45 years at that time after the war was over. I stopped the buggy, got out and held the line and told her to 'go get the flag.' "

Later, Murray charged an Altus insurance man supporting Cruce circulated the story that "Murray refused to march in the parade until the Confederate flag was taken down." He said that political canard "lost me thousands of votes throughout the state," and although the insurance man became a secondary state official for four decades, Murray listed him as one of the "two I have never been able to forgive." Twenty years later, Murray had the pleasure of trouncing him in another gubernatorial campaign.

J. B. A. Robertson of Chandler, former district judge, and F. E. Herring of Elk City, a member of the "Con Con," announced in 1910, but withdrew before the filing period. The field was completed with formal entries from Leslie P. Ross of Lawton and Brant Kirk of Durant.

With the great seal of state ensconced in Oklahoma City, Murray set off the fireworks with a challenge to the three other candidates for a series of joint debates. When the challenge was accepted, it was arranged to open the debates at Anadarko on July 5, with other dates on succeeding days in Enid, Oklahoma City, Ada and Durant.

Fred P. Branson of Muskogee, the Democratic state chairman and also chairman of the state election board, took alarm over the prospect of a knock-down-drag-out fight which would split the party in November. Officing at the Lee-Huckins hotel, only a few doors from the governor's quarters, it is likely that Branson conferred with Haskell before writing the candidates on June 27 to call off the debates.

"The committee of which I am chairman feels an interest in the campaign at least to this extent, that circumstances do not arise, if possible to be prevented, in which the candidates may be led to deal in personalities before the public," he wrote.

"The friction engendered by the meeting of minds in joint discussion often leads to expressions afterwards deprecated by the participants as well as the public.

"It seems there is not sufficient reason for the joint debates between you as candidates for governor on the Democratic ticket to outweigh the possibility of injurious results; therefore, believing it to the interest of the public, the party as a whole, and to you individually, it is requested that you do not engage in joint debates in this ante-primary campaign, and that the arrangements heretofore made to this end be cancelled."

Ignoring Branson's plea, Murray fired a July 4 salvo against the state election board which brought Haskell into the fray. Addressing a letter to Will Linn of Chickasha, the board's secretary, Murray declared:

"My understanding is that not a single member of this board is friendly to me in this campaign. Whether this be true or not, I do know that their associate member, Fred P. Branson, is and has been my personal and political enemy, growing mostly out of the contests in the first legislature over my advocacy of the guaranty bank law, the prohibition law and the measure providing for a gross production tax on oil.

"I wish to call your attention to the fact that in some of the counties of the state, the managers of one of my opponents, the Hon. Lee Cruce, are either inspectors or members of the county election board, and while in some of the other counties the election officers are my friends, the information has come to me, particularly in the case of Tillman county, that Mr. Branson has informed them that it was perfectly proper for said members of the county board to manage Mr. Cruce's campaign."

In his lengthy letter, Murray said it was "within the possibility of the county boards, by mutilating ballots, and otherwise, to change the result in those counties wherein strong partisans of the opposing candidates are in charge of the campaign.

"And I further submit that it is contrary to good principles of honestly-conducted elections for any manager of any candidate for public office to constitute any portion of the election machinery of the state, county or precinct, in view of the fact that when men are embroiled in the canvass, they are naturally disposed to believe that those who stand opposed to them in their community or section have been unfair in this contest, and this leads to the belief that it is proper to gain any advantage lost by use of the power of the count."

Murray asked permission to have his managers and friends designate watchers for the August 2 primary "with the view of guaranteeing a fair and honest count."

"I submit," he added, "that honest members of the election board everywhere will not object to being watched, and a dishonest member must be watched. I ask for nothing more than an honest election and a fair count . . . I wish to call your attention that from numerous sources the statement has been made that the result of this election 'has already been fixed;' that it matters not who wins it, 'Cruce will be counted in,' and you can clearly see by mutilating ballots, the result may be changed . . .

"I wish to state deliberately, that any man for any office who receives a nomination can and will be elected," Murray concluded, "but I want to say also that no man can be elected in Oklahoma who steals his nomination."

What Murray neglected to mention was an incident early in the session of the first legislature in which the speaker had "fired" Mrs. Branson, who had been employed as a reporter. Branson friends said the speaker had "cussed" the employee, and they even intimated the speaker sometimes spattered tobacco juice around her desk. At any rate, she found employment on the senate side, but the rift between Murray and Branson widened as the session progressed.

Noticeable, too, was the split between Murray and Haskell. It started in the July, 1907 secret session of the "Con Con" when Murray called the members into special meeting to make amendments conciliatory to Roosevelt. Haskell had won the primary the month before.

"After Haskell was nominated, he felt independent," Murray wrote in his Memoirs, "and in the midst of my discussion, when he raised the question, he blurted: 'Aw, shut up your damn nonsense.' I turned red in the face with chagrin and anger, and hotly replied with oaths: 'That is not what you called it when you were a candidate in the primary . . . If you do not continue to stand for what you stood for in the convention in open session, and what you authorized me to say you stood for . . . I will go out of this convention fighting you and favoring the Republican nominee as loyally and as enthusiastically as I aided your nomination.' "

Not many had known of this exchange between Murray and Haskell, but now the governor adroitly hoisted "Alfalfa Bill" on a barbed pen.

"I believe you will concede that during the pending primary, wherein you and Hon. Lee Cruce seek the Democratic nomination for governor, I have refrained from taking part, and I would not now desire to be understood as replying to your letter with any disposition whatever to have it affect the pending primary," Haskell wrote.

"But as all will understand, the members of this supreme election board are appointed by me, and I am, therefore, answerable to the people of this state for the integrity and proper official conduct for each and every member of the board . . . as it is my duty to uphold them when they are right and to condemn or even remove them from office, when they are wrong. Therefore, in a spirit of friendship, but with a determination to protect the public service against any improper practices, I feel it my duty to call upon you to furnish me with any evidence of improper conduct as to any of the members of said board that may come to your notice.

"I can readily understand that in the heat of a campaign, many stories are set afloat, and come to the ears of all of us, that upon inquiry prove to be idle gossip, and without foundation. I selected every member of this state election board, both Republicans and Democrats, from men who bear the reputation for the strictest honesty and efficiency, and after the most careful inquiry into the matters stated in your letter to Mr. Linn, I still feel that there is absolutely no cause for an attack upon Mr. Branson or any other member of the board."

Then Haskell quoted the page numbers in the house journal recording Branson's vote in favor of the guaranty law, the prohibition bill and the gross production tax.

"If these record facts have been misstated to you from the mouth of reckless gossip, it would be much easier for the idle gossip to have misstated to you of which no official record exists . . . I am positive from a most careful observation and inquiry that in assailing the integrity of Mr. Branson, you have acted on gossip, wholly groundless and utterly untruthful."

With reference to counters, Haskell sank the barb.

"I find that the election law as it existed prior to the act of the first legislature permitted a candidate to designate any elector of the precinct to be present at the canvassing of the vote cast, but the first legislature, wherein you presided as speaker in the house of representatives, amended this law, and therein provided that no person except the precinct canvassing board should be allowed within 50 feet of the official counters when the vote was being canvassed. I am sure that you must have thought that a proper law, or you never would have voted for its adoption."

The first debate was held in the district courtroom at Anadarko on a hot afternoon. Each candidate was allotted one hour, and long before the marathon was over, the initial crowd of 200 had dwindled more than half. The discussions in retrospect are illuminating for pointing up the drivel that influences elections.

W. F. Kerr, an *Oklahoman* reporter, took nearly two columns to describe the meeting. It is one of the best contemporary reports, but it is well to remember the *Oklahoman*—under editorship of State Sen. Roy E. Stafford—was supporting Cruce. Dan W. Peery of Carnegie presided and Rep. R. I. Glover of Chickasha was timekeeper.

Kirk led off. Familiarly known as "General" because of his active participation in Confederate affairs, Kirk stood firmly against resubmission of the prohibition question—in opposition to Ross. He charged Murray and Cruce with being astraddle the fence, asserting:

"You wouldn't pull them into a fight with a log chain; you couldn't blow them into the fight with dynamite."

Then he touched on a burning issue:

"I am a better farmer than Bill Murray. The farm lost a good hand when it lost me. Murray wasn't worth $5.50 a month on the farm. I can take a one-hand coffee mill and grind all the alfalfa and cane these other candidates raised in all their lives. I could have been a horny-handed son of toil now if I had rubbed my palm with a corncob for campaign purposes, as some of these candidates have done."

Referring to the "grandfather clause"—a proposed amendment to disfranchise Negro voters—Kirk said he "understood the gentleman from Johnston county was against it. I understand he said in his speech in Oklahoma City that it was the rankest partisan doctrine. I understand he is on the right side now."

Murray, introduced next, said he was aware "I am in the enemy's country." Discussing the proposed amendment, he declared he favored the disfranchisement of every Negro, and would give every white man the right to vote. He referred to his opponents as "national bank Democrats," "Santa Fe railroad Democrats" and "Brewery Democrats," and declared himself to be "a constitutional Democrat."

Lee Cruce he referred to as "A French gentleman," and he argued that Cruce had no right to be governor because he didn't help make the constitution and the laws. He called Ross the "clansman"—the latter had the support of the Sons of Washington—and lauded Gov. Douglas H. Johnston of the Chickasaws. Lifting his 10-year-old son, Massena, to the table, he said the boy was descended from Bancroft and from Gen. Albert Sidney Johnston, the Confederate general killed at the battle of Shiloh.

Murray said he had been charged with being a drunkard. He called upon the audience to view his features and testify to the fact that "my face is not bloated, and my nose is not red."

Much of Murray's time was devoted to advocating the Torrens land system, a law in effect in Australia, to guarantee land titles. Murray had advocated the Torrens system in the Constitutional Convention; failing there, he prevailed on the first legislature to submit it to a vote of the people. It was defeated in the 1908 general election, but in his Altus speech—printed for distribution—Murray had declared:

"I had rather have added to the laws of Oklahoma the Torrens land system in its full vigor than to be made governor of the state, and I shall risk gaining sufficient votes from the great body of the people who need this provision for every vote I lose by reason of its advocacy."

Murray gave this explanation of the Torrens land system in his Memoirs:

"It, in brief, was devised by Richard Robert Torrens, in Australia, and is designed to take the place of abstracts of title by the transfer of titles to land similar to the sale of stocks in a corporation, on the books of the company. When thus transferred, the state stands behind the title. It recites every condition of the title on the face of the land certificate.

"If a piece of land be held in fee by one man, and he executes a lease to another, and gives a lien to borrow money, once, twice, or three conditions, on the land certificate, and each of these transactions is recorded on the face of the land certificate, and as the claim is paid, or the lease expire, the officer gives him a new certificate, eliminating that condition of the title; so that any man, whether lawyer or not, can tell every condition of the land title.

"Naturally the abstracters and the lawyers fought it, because you cannot imagine a suit on land under it, except on a disputed boundary, or in probate of minors, and of estates. It was adopted in Chicago necessarily after the burning of Chicago. It is in force in the state of Maine, Massachusetts, and in Mexico where the records show that at one time they had an abstract that weighed 500 pounds. As a country grows older the greater the volume of the abstract. That is not the title, but the evidence of title, and the 'evidence' may be false."

A similar system is in vogue today for transferring title to a motor vehicle; every time the vehicle is sold, the state issues a new title. But as Murray pointed out, abstracters and lawyers, in particular, fought the Torrens system and defeated its adoption.

The constitution had exempted certain Indian lands from taxation, but Murray exhibited his tax receipts showing he had paid taxes on his Indian lands. He reiterated a former statement that "the poor old darky should not be made an issue in this campaign," but declared for the grandfather clause.

Ross was fighting "Haskellism." Going to Lawton in the Kiowa-

Comanche opening of 1901 as register of the land office, he had unseated J. Roy Williams, co-author of the guaranty fund law, to win a place in the second legislature. He charged Murray with being active in enactment of laws to give the governor autocratic power "to thwart the will of the people."

Citing 27 state institutions, Ross said there were 51 representatives in the house from institutional counties. Since the governor held veto power over institutional appropriations, he asserted the chief executive could control the house by winning only four additional votes through job promises. He advocated the election of bank commissioner, game warden and other officers now appointive "in order that the governor would not be able to build up a machine that would permit him to dictate his successor in office."

Then, with a parting shot at Haskell, whose wife frequently took her knitting and sat in the governor's outer office, Ross invited the audience to assist him at the capitol where "my wife will not be darning socks in the executive offices, or making lye soap in the backyard."

"I am a Democrat and despise the autocrat, under whatever name he travels," Ross shouted. "I am persuaded this autocratic power in the governor can never be taken away until some man is elected governor who favors its destruction.

"The sooner its destruction is attempted, the easier it will be. The sooner it is destroyed, the better it will be for the governor and the people."

Ross also called for another vote on the prohibition question. Pointing out that "a condition was imposed upon Oklahoma in the Enabling Act never before imposed on any other state," he said the people should be given a chance to decide the issue.

When Cruce arose to speak, *The Oklahoman* reported "the audience went wild with applause." He announced that "not one word would fall from my lips that would make the women's cheeks blush with shame."

"You have heard a Republican speech, and a Socialist speech," he said, "and I propose to make a Democratic speech. I have come here to help the democracy of Caddo county, and not to deride. When the time shall come when I am afraid to draw the sword in defense of the party, you will not find me asking for any office. Don't get the idea that there is anything in the party that we should not be proud of. I am here to defend my party, and not one word has been said before me in the party's defense."

He took a potshot at Joe McNeal, the Guthrie banker who was seeking the Republican nomination. Denying McNeal charges of extravagance in the state government, Cruce declared:

"It has cost $5,000,000 more to operate the Republican state of Kansas than it has to operate Democratic Oklahoma, yet they want us to turn Oklahoma over to the Republicans."

Cruce defended the Haskell administration, and added, "if you want a man elevated to standard bearer of the party in this state who will not defend that administration, don't you put me there. I don't propose to say in these discussions one single thing that will lose my party one single vote, and if these discussions degenerate into personal matters, I propose to withdraw from these debates, as I have a perfect right to do."

He told of how he fought for the constitution, which he considered "the best in the world," making speeches throughout the state. Cruce exhibited receipts showing that the taxes had been been paid on all his lands, the total amount being approximately $1,000 on lands aggregating 500 acres, while Murray paid less than $300 on 1,400 acres. He declared that if any one of the other candidates won the nomination, "he will get Lee Cruce's support" and he would never say one word that would be a cudgel in the hands of the Republican party.

As for the Torrens land system, Cruce asserted that if adopted, "in the eastern part of the state those land grafters would own two-thirds of these lands in two years. There are some 30,000 suits involving Indian lands on that side, and under this system the state would have to guarantee every one of those titles. If such cases were fought in the U. S. supreme court and a decision given against the state, the state would have to make them good. The system would bankrupt the state."

Cruce said he voted for prohibition in 1907, and never had reason to be sorry. He declared the law "is as well enforced as in any other state, and if the people have the right sentiment to make the demand, the law will be enforced as well as any other law."

The speeches at Enid were largely a repetition of the talks at Anadarko. Murray did declare against woman suffrage, which was being proposed in a new initiative petition sponsored by the Woman Suffrage association. When the candidates reached Oklahoma City, about 500 turned out for the meeting in convention hall.

A woman in the audience asked Cruce if he favored woman

suffrage.

"In reply," the pro-Cruce *Oklahoman* reported, "he said there is not one feather's weight of argument against it, that women have as much right to vote as men, that at the rate girls are being educated—three girls to one boy—the women soon will be better able to take care of the government than men, but that he opposed women voting solely on the grounds of sentiment, because he thought woman's place was in the home and in the society of nobler and higher ideals than those which men are chosen to follow."

At Ada, Murray and Cruce clashed when the former charged that A. C. Cruce had been a candidate for office at Ardmore in the spring on the independent ticket. Lee Cruce arose and told Murray he was making "a deliberate misstatement." Murray insisted that he was correct, and gave his authority. Cruce remained standing.

"If there is one word of truth in what you say, I will withdraw from this race, and if you will withdraw if the statement is false," Cruce challenged. "Will you admit that I am a Democrat?" asked Murray. Cruce admitted as much, and Murray withdrew the statement.

About 1,200 attended the debate, in a tabernacle. When Kirk arose to speak, he complained of the heat and was advised he might remove his coat.

"I'll never do that," he retorted. "I might be taken for Bill Murray."

The debates ended at Durant on Saturday, July 9, where the time limit was doubled. With each candidate allotted two hours, the meeting was split into morning and afternoon sessions.

In a campaign review on July 29, Cruce said: "I have steadfastly maintained that the supreme issue in this state is this—shall the Democratic party remain in control of the affairs of this state?"

Cruce won easily on August 2 with 54,262 votes, a margin of 14,000 over Murray, but until his dying day "Alfalfa Bill" always contended he had been "counted out." Immediately after the primary, he fired a blast at the election board, asserting that a shortage of ballots in "Murray counties" cut down his total. Haskell intimates, on the other hand, would give a knowing wink and imply that Murray had contributed to his own defeat by alienating the election officials. They said he had taken the "bait" of gossip in questioning the honesty of the officials at the outset.

Ross finished third, with 26,792, while Kirk fell far behind with only 2,514. The Republicans also nominated a banker, Joe McNeal of

Guthrie, and thus the fall campaign became a contest between "the national bankers," an unusual combination in a rugged, pioneer state.

Incidentally, the secondary state officers found their way around constitutional prohibitions against succeeding terms in certain offices. Bill Cross, barred from re-election as secretary of state, filed for state auditor; M. E. Trapp, the auditor, filed for treasurer, while Cross' assistant, Leo Meyer, ran for secretary of state.

Cross was on his death bed in St. Anthony's hospital in Oklahoma City on election day, and anxious supporters stood fearfully hoping he would live until the polls closed. He died about 6:30 a. m. on Wednesday as the newspapers reported his nomination. A few days later, Haskell appointed a fellow townsman, Thomas P. Smith, to succeed Cross.

Meyer, defeated for secretary of state, later was selected by the central committee to take Cross' place on the ballot for auditor. Trapp, who boasted in his campaign that he had defeated a Republican Negro opponent for Logan county clerk in 1904—prima facie evidence of "white supremacy"—lost the treasurer's race to Robert Dunlop of Newkirk.

But the pattern had been set. Henceforth, every four years, Oklahoma voters would see statehouse veterans "swapping keys" to stay on the public pay roll.

CHAPTER XV

For White Men Only

OKLAHOMA'S white males set a record for gallantry in 1910. Before the year was out, they would disfranchise most of the Negroes and defeat woman suffrage. It was an era not only of white supremacy, but of male supremacy!

To avoid the tide of opposition votes in presidential elections—Oklahoma has gone Republican in four presidential years since statehood—the first governor's term had been cut short. Thus, Oklahoma elects state officers in the so-called "off" year. At statehood, most Negro voters were registered Republicans; if they could be denied the ballot, Oklahoma would be safe for Democracy—with a capital "D."

Rebuffed in early attempts to invalidate the Jim Crow law, Negroes faced the loss of voting privileges under a series of measures passed by the second legislature including Senate Concurrent Resolution No. 31 by Sen. L. K. Taylor of Chickasha. The legislature reduced the time for circulating initiative petitions from 90 to 60 days then "suggested" in the resolution a popular drive to write the "grandfather clause" into the constitution by initiative petition.

This was a brazen attempt to deprive Negroes of the right of suffrage under the guise of prescribing an "educational test" by declaring:

"No person shall be registered as an elector of this state, or be allowed to vote in any election held herein, unless he be able to read and write any section of the Constitution of the State of Oklahoma; but no person who was, on Jan. 1, 1866, or at any time prior thereto, entitled to vote under any form of government, or who at that time resided in some foreign nation, and no lineal descendant of such person, shall be denied the right to register and vote because of his inability to read and write sections of such constitution."

In other words, the ignorant white man, native or immigrant, should have the right to vote; the Negro must qualify by written test in the hands of precinct election officials, many little better versed than he.

The Democratic state central committee, headed by Branson,

started circulating initiative petitions in April and filed 43,140 signatures in early June. *The Oklahoman* for June 19, 1910, carried Branson's statement that the proposed amendment "is copied from the constitution in the state of North Carolina, which provision was adopted in 1900, and after litigation in the courts, the validity of the same was upheld by the highest tribunal of the nation."

"The question as to whether the amendment, when adopted, will be valid, having already been passed upon by the supreme court of the United States, the only question remaining for the people in the state of Oklahoma to consider is whether this amendment, if adopted, will tend to increase the wholesome condition of our social status, our property values and our political ability," he added.

Then, quoting a speech by Abraham Lincoln at Charlston, Ill., in September, 1858, "that I am not, nor ever have been, in favor of making voters or jurors of Negroes," Branson continued:

"Indiscriminate suffrage in the hands of the Negro is inconsistent with the lack of the right on his part to hold office indiscriminately. If he has one, he can with as much political propriety have the other, and you are face to face with a political condition which, when the Negro population becomes large enough, will be satisfied only by the political offices being filled by persons of African descent."

Lending impetus to Branson's remark was the presence in the second legislature of the only Negro elected to that body since statehood. He was A. C. Hamlin of Guthrie, a Republican, serving as state representative.

"By way of parenthesis," Branson added, "I wonder how Abraham Lincoln would feel if he walked into the Oklahoma legislature and saw the representative of the Republican party in the lower house, the party of which he is the exponent, counseling with a Negro representative of Logan county on matters which involved the social condition, the property values and the political stability of the great new commonwealth of Oklahoma?

"Eliminate this question by adopting this amendment, then the white people of Oklahoma who have blazed out the path and made clear the way for building well a great commonwealth, can govern Oklahoma with policies of progress, fraternal love and social equality, and racial questions and political fights will be eliminated."

Republicans and Socialists filed vigorous protests, challenging the proposed amendment as unconstitutional. James A. Harris of Wagoner,

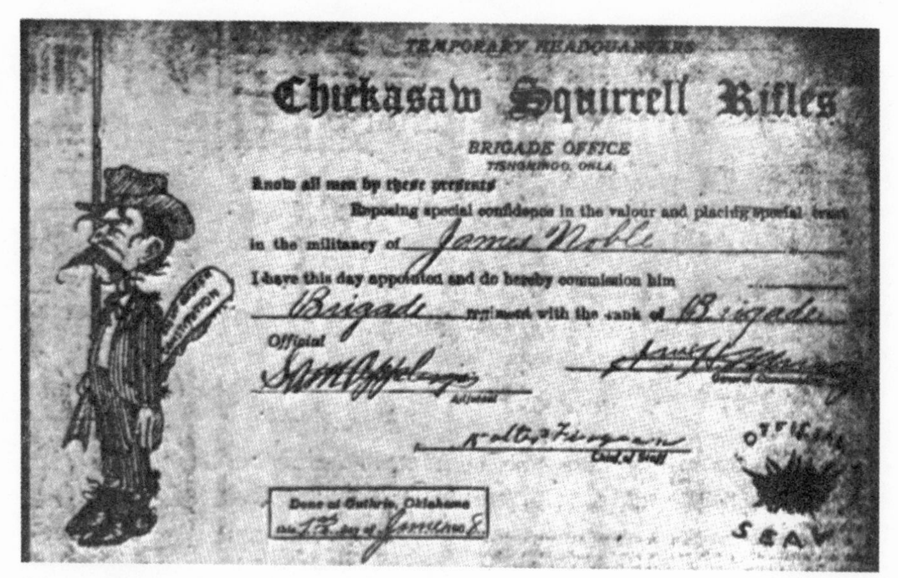

TEMPORARY HEADQUARTERS

Chickasaw Squirrell Rifles

BRIGADE OFFICE

TISHOMINGO, OKLA.

Know all men by these presents

Reposing special confidence in the valour and placing special trust in the militancy of James Noble

I have this day appointed and do hereby commission him Brigade regiment with the rank of Brigade

Official

Adjutant

General Commanding

Chief of Staff

Done at Guthrie, Oklahoma this 17th day of January

OFFICIAL SEAL

A commission for Jim Noble, faithful Negro follower, was circulated by opposition to "prove" Murray's apostasy toward "grandfather clause" in 1910 campaign.

the Republican state chairman, declared the purpose of the amendment, "while it purports to prescribe an educational test, it is to disfranchise persons of African descent, also the descendants of persons who were formerly held in slavery."

A more vehement protest came from the executive committee of the Socialist party, with Patrick S. Nagle of Kingfisher and Oscar Ameringer of Oklahoma City among the members. Other protests were filed in the name of Sampson Smith, an 80-year-old former slave, and other Negroes.

Senate Bill 26 had passed the legislature with the emergency clause and the state supreme court held it therefore was not subject to attack by referendum. Repulsed on this front, Nagle and his committee filed with the secretary of state a biting argument against adopting the petition. Referring to SB 26—and the language suggests Ameringer as the author—they declared:

"This is the most infamous piece of legislation passed by the reactionaries now in power. In the folds of this bill are concealed not only the fangs of the rattlesnake, but the knife of the assassin . . . When they passed and declared this bill to be the law of the state, they plunged a butcher knife into the bowels of the initiative and referendum and turned it around. There is nothing left of the initiative and referendum in this state but a new-made grave. If there are those who weep and wish to erect a monument over the remains, I suggest this epitaph: 'Assassinated by legislative chicanery and executive debauchery with judicial sanction.'"

But SB 26 and companion measures by the legislature were necessary for the scheme which the proponents had in mind to record every ballot cast—except those deliberately marked otherwise—for the amendment. These tactics would reverse the usual procedure in which the so-called "silent vote" counts against the measure.

Nagle denounced the trickery by which the measure would be submitted.

"With the 'suggestion' bill," he pointed out, "it is provided that 'For the Amendment' shall be printed in an inconspicuous place and without any distinguishing marks, and if you do not hunt it up and strike it out with your pencil, you are voted for the 'suggested' amendment."

Although Branson was called as a witness, legal objections thwarted most interrogations. He did testfy, however, that "my part in initiating this proposition was to carry out the intention of the legislature as incorporated in the law." Overruling protests, Cross sustained the petitions June 16. In record time, the supreme court six days later upheld his ruling.

"The constitutionality or validity of a proposed initiated measure cannot be determined on a hearing before the secretary of state," the court held. Haskell promptly issued his proclamation placing the question on the August 2 primary ballot where it was adopted, 134,443 to 106,222.

When the valadity of the amendment was attacked in the state supreme court that fall, the court upheld the measure in a decision by Justice Williams on October 26—just two weeks before the general election. Alabama-born Williams relied in part upon the Scriptures in pursuing an unusual line of thought:

"To say, because plaintiff (a former slave) or his ancestors . . . were not entitled to vote under any organized form of government on or prior to Jan. 1, 1866 . . . that said amendment discriminates against them on account of race or color, is as unfounded as to say that a property qualification discriminates on account of previous condition of servitude for the reason that . . . a slave could not acquire property any more than he could vote . . .

"That is a qualification based upon a reason; that is, that any person who was entitled to vote under a form of government on or prior to said date is still presumed to be qualified to exercise such right, and the presumption follows as to his offspring—that is, *that the virtues and intelligence of the ancestor will be imputed to his descendants, just as the iniquity of the fathers may be visited upon the children to the third of fourth generation.* But as to those who were not entitled to vote under any form of government on said date, or at any prior time, and their descendants, there is no presumption in favor of their qualifications, and the burden is on them to show themselves qualified."

But the U. S. supreme court took a dim view of this logic. Five years went by, however, before that tribunal struck down the "grandfather clause" on June 21, 1915, in an appeal prosecuted by federal authority.

"We have difficulty in finding words to more clearly demonstrate the conviction we entertain that this standard has the characteristic which the government attributed to it than does the mere statement of the text," wrote Chief Justice White. "It is true it contains no express words of exclusion from the standard which it establishes . . . but the standard itself inherently brings that result into existence since it is based purely upon a period of time before the enactment of the fifteenth amendment and makes that period the controlling and dominant test of suffrage . . .

"Certainly it cannot be said that there was any peculiar necromancy in the time which engendered attributes affecting the qualification to vote which would not exist at another and different period unless the fifteenth amendment was in view."

So, after five years, Negroes regained the right to vote. For the moment, however, they were stymied despite the advice of John Embry, U. S. district attorney at Guthrie, that they might qualify by presenting affidavits at the polls as to their ability to read and write. Haskell called on election officials to enforce the law in the general election and Branson on behalf of the Democratic state central committee offered a $50 reward "for evidence leading to the arrest and conviction for violation of the same."

Speaking in a tent at Muskogee on the eve of the November 8 election, Haskell "told the Negroes, and there was a large number present to hear him, that they need not expect to vote next Tuesday unless they can read and write, and that the election inspectors are the sole judge of their qualifications," the *Oklahoman* reported.

"Of course," said the governor, "you will not be expected to read with the faculty of an elocutionist, but I expect you to do as well as a professor, at least. And while you will not have to write a copper-plate hand, you will have to make it perfectly legible."

Meantime, the Woman Suffrage association was circulating initiative petitions for an amendment granting women the right to vote. Ineligible to sign themselves, the women—with generous assistance from hundreds of willing husbands—faced the task of getting men voters to sign the petitions. Both the Democrats and Republicans were silent on woman suffrage in their state platforms, but the Socialists were "strong and open" advocates of the cause. The State Federation of Labor also espoused woman suffrage. Ira M. Mullinax, writing in *Sturm's Oklahoma Magazine,* told the story of their efforts:

"Thousands of names must be secured, and every name must be that of a qualified voter. Dr. Ruth A. Gay, laying aside her professional duties, took charge of the clerical work. Mrs. J. A. Burt contributed her services and paid all the incidental expenses. Mrs. Adelia C. Stephens traveled over the state, securing signatures, as did many other advocates of the cause. And when they had finished, the big petition had been signed by 38,586 voters.

"When the petition was offered to the late Bill Cross, secretary of state, for filing, it was found that women had 'no political existence' in the state of Oklahoma, and that there was no law under which a woman might be given the receipt for the petition, as required by law. Only a man could act in this capacity, and just as the women were on the point of despair, J. Luther Langston, secretary of the State Federation of Labor, came to their rescue and had the receipt made out in his name. Even then the petitions were attacked upon the ground that they were insufficient, but after a hearing Secretary Cross held the petitions sufficient and valid in all respects and they were allowed to be placed on file."

Haskell ordered the question submitted at the general election.

Mrs. Ida Porter-Boyer, a national leader in the suffrage movement, came down from Philadelphia to serve as secretary in the state headquarters. An *Oklahoman* reporter who interviewed Mrs. Boyer found her anything but the cartoonist's idea of a suffragette.

"She was dressed in a white summer gown, trimmed only with some Venitian point lace. Contrary to expectation, I noticed that buttons and placards were conspicuous by their absence. On her waist was a fraternity pin which I afterwards learned belonged to her son, a graduate of Harvard University," he wrote on July 3.

Mrs. Boyer outlined her arguments for the ballot:

"By giving a woman suffrage, you do not take away her beauty, her charms nor her motherhood. You add to these by giving her an interest in your affairs, and in the affairs of the nation.

"Because a woman votes, it does not mean that a man may love her less. It does not detract from her ability as a housewife. It does not hide her manifold other charms in any manner. I often hear the argument that association at the polls with men would cause women to be coarse. Let me say here, that conditions that exist today could not exist if women voted . . .

"I want clean streets, and I want my boy to have opportunities. I want a safe and sane Fourth, I want clean politics, not because I am desirous of holding office, but because of my personal feelings and because of my boy. There are thousands of other mothers in the same position. We cannot get them under the present regime. It must be through woman suffrage, and in no other way."

And what about the suffragettes? Mullinax described them this way:

"Among the really prominent workers, only two or three are unmarried. Most of the others have families, some of them large enough to fit the standards even of Theodore Roosevelt. For example, one of them has eight and another eleven children, yet they, like their coworkers, have found time both for the cause of suffrage and the proper rearing of these interesting families."

Mrs. Boyer recognized the handicap of the "silent vote" from those too indifferent to mark their ballots in a general election.

"While we realize that against us will be arrayed the liquor element, the crooked politician who fears the votes of decent women will put him out of office, and a large foreign vote, on the other hand the Socialists are for us to a man, while practically all the better informed of the laboring classes will vote for suffrage," she said. "The greatest disadvantage is the fact that the amendment comes up at a general election. This means that it must receive a majority of all votes cast, and since so many voters are apt to disregard constitutional amendments, we shall no doubt lose a good many votes for this reason."

The women and their allies waged a determined campaign, but

the amendment lost by wide margin, 88,808 in favor to 128,928 against. In the primary, the white males had disfranchised the Negro; by denying women the ballot in November, they had, in effect, put a sign on the voting booth, "For White Men Only!"

Cruce won the governorship, defeating McNeal by a vote of 120,-218 to 99,527. The Socialists, who had polled 9,740 in 1907, surged upwards to 24,707 votes for J. T. Cumbie, their nominee. The Socialists were on the march, but the Democrats were in control. The entire Democratic state ticket rode into office with Cruce.

Haskell delivered his final message to the legislature on Jan. 7, 1911. The Third legislature, which had wound up the special session on the capital location in 18 days, convened in regular session January 3, but the governor's message was delayed to await reports from some of the state departments. Haskell purposely avoided recommendations, telling the lawmakers that was the prerogative of the new governor, but the message reflected pride in the growth of Oklahoma and the accomplishments of his administration.

"In the many earlier states there are found no parallel and no precedent to guide us in our work," he asserted. "In Oklahoma, we were called upon to unite two distinct territories, one wholly unorganized, with a combined population of 1,414,000 people and with an aggregate corporate wealth of $250,000,000. To harmonize these two territories, organize locally and generally into a single state, to consider the demands and necessities of such vast population and meet the contention of such vast corporate wealth, to deal justly with all and bring order out of such chaotic condition was an undertaking without precedent, requiring patience, zeal and industry without limit and to which those most willing for honorable public service would not knowingly aspire.

"Three years have passed, and we find our population has increased 243,000 people; our taxable wealth has increased $235,000,000; our commerce and manufacturing industries almost 300 percent, and a clear index to the financial growth of the state is found in our individual deposits in the banks of the state." Reduced to round numbers, in table form, Haskell quoted these figures:

	1907	1911
State banks	$17,000,000	$ 56,000,000
National banks	38,000,000	46,000,000
	$55,000,000	$102,000,000

"The dawn of statehood found us in the midst of a 30-day holiday, officially proclaimed for the purpose of relieving the banks of the territory from the necessity of paying depositors on demand," the governor continued, "and by reason of the holiday proclamation, banks were privileged to make their own rules, if they cared to transact business or pay depositors at all. As a result, it was the general practice to limit the depositor's demands, for his own money, to $5 or $10 per day.

"This condition suggested the necessity for a revision of the banking laws, not only of the states but of the nation; and Oklahoma, ever mindful of her duty to her citizens, immediately took up the consideration of a banking law, such as contemplated by our constitution, under which banking might be treated as a semi-public business, where the rights of the public and the rights and privilege of the banker should both be fairly considered."

Recounting passage of the Depositors' Guaranty Fund law in 1907, Haskell said the law since that time, "has been subjected to the most vicious assaults and untruthful criticism." He continued:

"In brief, the results speak for the law. No depositor in any state bank in Oklahoma has ever lost a dollar in the entire three years, or been refused when he demanded his money, at any business hour of any business day of the year.

"Never have the services of a policeman been required to aid in the conduct of the state banking business in Oklahoma. We have had our bank failures, and doubtless always will have so long as human nature remains unchanged. And it is for the purpose of protecting the public against loss and disaster that Oklahoma has a law to successfully manage and liquidate insolvent banks; and where the answer to the anxious depositor, in a failed bank operating under other laws, when he may get his money invariably is: 'God only knows,' under Oklahoma state banking law, the answer to such inquiry is, 'you can get it now.' "

Haskell said 85 percent of the losses under the guaranty law had been occasioned "by the failure of a single aggregation of men controlling a number of banks . . . including two large national and one of the largest state banks, and several smaller banks."

"To show the efficiency of the Oklahoma state banking law," he added, "I call your attention to its notable test in liquidating the Columbia Bank & Trust Co. with its $3,294,000 of liabilities, at a total expense of $13,775.24, accomplished almost complete in five months, as compared with the settlement of the failed Capitol National Bank of Guthrie, with total liabilities under $700,000, which after six years is still incomplete, although over $55,000 expenses have been incurred and paid, and the depositors in this six-year period have had small instalments aggregating less than two-thirds of the principal."

Haskell reported total assessments for the guaranty fund through Dec. 31, 1910, at $840,392.23. After deducting refunds and adjustments totaling $21,551.58, the net stood at $818,740.65.

As he spoke, the governor said the total cash balance of the fund stood at $333,787.68. On the basis of his figures, the total cost of bank failures was slightly less than $500,000. Having delivered his swan song, Haskell prepared to participate in a welcome to his successor. Although the senate in the brief special session on capital location had rejected a house bill appropriating $5,000 for Lee Cruce's inaugural ceremony, the Ardmore banker, accompanied by scores of friends and a military band, came to Oklahoma City by special train on Monday to take the helm of government. The ceremony took place at noon in the presence of members of the legislature and a throng of well wishers in Convention hall.

CHAPTER XVI

Sequel

AFTER watching his successor installed, C. N. Haskell returned home to Muskogee. He had disposed of his commercial interests nearly five years before, when he was elected to the Constitutional Convention. Retiring as governor, he let it be known that he was practically "broke," but as usual, Haskell was resourceful.

Moreover, the Muskogee Commercial club had extended a heart-warming invitation the summer before. The club adopted a resolution in late August recounting that "Governor Haskell since 1902 has been prominently identified with the upbuilding of his home city. His genius has been largely responsible for the enviable position Muskogee holds today as the second city in the State of Oklahoma," and it urged the governor "to come home and take his place with us as a builder of a greater Muskogee."

The *Oklahoma State Capital*, waging battle on Haskell to the bitter end, carried this banner across its front page on inaugural day:

"The King Is Dead—Welcome Gov. Cruce."

After adopting the welcoming resolution, members of the Commercial club subscribed $101,500 toward a $300,000 capital fund for the Grand River Water Power Co. The sponsors outlined a plan to place Haskell at the head of the company which would start dredging operations to make the Arkansas navigable. This was a program close to Haskell's heart, and years before he had demonstrated the feasibility of water transportation with the Molly D.

The water development program failed to materialize, however, and soon the former governor was in the real estate development business. He promoted the Monticello sub-division in east Muskogee, building his own fine home in the division. He also returned to his first love, rail promotion, with an interurban line from Muskogee to Ft. Gibson.

Turning again to politics, Haskell made a disastrous race for United States senator in 1912, losing to Robert L. Owen, 44,483 to 80,204. Then came an invitation from Harry F. Sinclair, the one-time traveling salesman who had become a titan in the oil business. Sinclair prevailed on Haskell to move to New York as his personal attorney. With five years of schooling at the hands of Sinclair, Haskell launched his Middle States Oil Co. in 1917. Riding the crest of the oil boom in World War I, the former governor was soon in the millionaire class.

Town Topics, a weekly magazine published in New York, traced the rapid growth of the company from net earnings of $20,558 in its first six months to $114,313 for the first half year of 1919, and a record $8,752,375 for the year 1920. When Scott Ferris, the genial congressman from Lawton, was defeated for United States senator in the Harding landslide of 1920, Haskell organized a subsidiary and placed Ferris in the presidency. Another subsidiary was headed by James V. McClintic, the seventh district congressman.

Then the bubble burst, and Haskell saw his personal fortune swept away. He always blamed Andrew Mellon, the Pittsburgh financier and controlling force behind the Gulf Oil Co., for the collapse of Middle States. After receiving an invitation from President Oberon of Mexico to help write the oil laws for that country, Haskell came in conflict with Mellon. The government slapped an $8,000,000 tax lien on Middle States and threw the company into receivership. Although the tax suit ultimately was settled for $160,000, Middle States was wrecked.

Haskell's next venture, the promotion of a toll road in Mexico, resulted from his acquaintance with President Calles, Oberon's successor. His plan was to link Matamoras with Tampico. The project proved a forerunner of the Pan-American highway.

During the halcyon days in New York, Haskell struck up a personal acquaintance with Roosevelt. The latter, fretting because the Wilson administration would not let him head an army division in France, took lunch about once a month with the "blackguard" he had sought to put "in stripes."

"Nothwithstanding their intense enmity, no two men in public life in America are more alike than Haskell and Roosevelt," wrote O. P. Sturm in a review of the Haskell administration in 1911. Now the two became fast friends and over the luncheon table, "Teddy" confided that he had not meant for the government attorneys to go so far in the lot fraud prosecutions.

In March, 1917, Roosevelt took an unusual step to modify the record. At his request, Mott, the attorney who had uncovered the lot cases for the Creek Indians, entered into the files of the Interior Department an apology to the former governor of Oklahoma.

Taken ill while visiting in Oklahoma City in 1933, Haskell died on July 7. He was buried in Greenhill cemetery in Muskogee. His grave is the only one of a former governor marked officially by the state. The late Bower Broaddus of Muskogee, then a state senator, sponsored a resolution in the legislature for a memorial shaft, which was erected in 1938. Mrs. Haskell died July 13, 1940, and was buried beside her husband.

Haskell provoked violent criticism, but friend and foe, those who knew him best, agreed that he was a tireless worker and resourceful to the utmost.

"The secret of his success is due to his adaptability to ideas and conditions and his never tiring energy," wrote Walter Ferguson as the Haskell administration ended. "During the three years he has been governor, he has slept less than any man in the state.

"When honest people were in bed, Haskell was conferring with some politician or figuring out some political scheme. The only defeat of consequence he has suffered in the state, was the failure of his Putnam City plan, and I was not in the least surprised to see in the papers the next day that 'the governor always favored a close-in site.' How well he adapts himself to conditions is manifest in the fact that he started in at the Constitutional Convention as the uncompromising enemy of Oklahoma City and wound up at the close of his term as governor by delivering to that city the capital of the state."

Henry S. Johnston, back in the state senate, was selected to pay official tribute on the senate floor after Haskell's death. Recalling Haskell's role in the statehood fight, his colleague of the "Con Con" added:

"As a delegate he was a diplomatic organizer, a great harmonizer, a pacificator, and the friend and confidant of the entire membership. He wrote many of its sections and took active part in every deliberation.

"As first governor of Oklahoma, he did more than occupy a station. He comprehended those broad principles and a mastership of the almost infinite detail essential to sound policy and to wise administration in a situation requiring profound understanding and fraught with infinite peril. His administrative triumphs were a literal example of the 'survival of the fittest in the midst of a hostile environment.' "

Mrs. Johnston, who had served as a stenographer when Haskell was governor, added her bit:

"With boundless energy he worked 20 hours a day, giving himself and every ounce of his capacity to the public welfare. He cared not for place, except as a means of service."

Although Murray and Haskell drifted apart in the first legislature, "Alfalfa Bill" in his Memoirs declared Haskell "outstanding in some particulars. He was as economical as any governor we ever had; generally fair; was a good governor for the Indians as well as for the whites; was neither a great lawyer, scholar nor learned, but possessed one of the keenest, practical minds you would find in a dozen states. His life had been spent in business principally as a contractor and railroad builder. He was daring in the extreme—daring even when the law forbade, as most men would 'shy' from."

Perhaps the best character analysis came from Paul Nesbitt, a veteran newspaperman. Nesbitt supported Cruce against Haskell in the first primary, but on the latter's invitation, joined the governor's staff. Writing in the *Chronicles* for June, 1936, Nesbitt observed:

"Charles N. Haskell possessed the very highest order of executive ability. Whether as governor of a state, builder of a railroad or head of a corporation, he perceived the essentials and vigorously pressed activities to accomplishment. He never encumbered himself with details—like a good general, he left details to subordinates. He was a born leader of men, and like leaders of men, inspired confidence and enthusiasm in others.

"He was not a profound lawyer, but he could draw from a profound lawyer enough information in an hour to guide him through hazardous cases. He was not a great statesman, but he grasped the essentials from association with statesmen and put into practice what students could never rise to perform. He relied heavily upon information of other men, but relied upon his own genius in the execution of whatever problems he had in hand.

"I do not mean to say that he never made mistakes. He was an intrepid and, at times, an impulsive fighter in any line of endeavor; and impulsiveness leads one into error. But even when he erred, he was to be feared, for he was resourceful in the utmost degree and often turned what appeared to be defeat into victory."

As irony would have it, the *Oklahoma State Capital* folded a year to the day from the date of Haskell's proclamation calling the special election for removing the capital. It is doubtful if Greer would have given his arch enemy the satisfaction of so symbolic a defeat if he had consulted the calendar. But on March 28, 1911, Greer announced that subscription lists and advertising contracts had been sold to the rival Democratic *Leader.*

"It is hard to part with the *State Capital,*" he wrote in a front page editorial. "It is my child. To me it has been a thing of flesh and blood. There has been a sentiment about it as sweet as a woman's love. The best years of my life have been devoted to it. Many cherished memories are bound up in it. Its files are an epitome of the history of Guthrie and Oklahoma . . .

"I came to Guthrie on its opening day. I was then a boy, full of youthful ambition. I have taken a keen interest in every moment of the city's growth. I love Guthrie with a warm affection. I have lost no faith in it. It will emerge from the shock of losing the capital of the state much stronger than ever."

Thus ended a saga of youthful venture which could have been written only in a pioneer territory. As a matter of fact, as Greer himself related in *Sturm's Oklahoma Magazine* years before, he had actually been a "sooner" in a day when the word carried opprobrium. Born July 21, 1862, in Leavenworth, Kan., Greer was the son of a Union Army captain. When the parents decided to move to Cowley county, Frank's father was so ill he rode in the back of the wagon. En route, one of the horses died. The family's plight was desperate, but Clotida Hilton Greer, the mother, was a determined soul and believed in prayer. She told the children that she would "draw a draft on the bank of Providence." Some passing settlers had abandoned an ox which was lame. Mrs. Greer nursed the animal, and when the ox had recovered, hitched it up with the remaining horse and continued her journey.

As a boy, Frank learned the printer's trade in Winfield; he also came to know the railroad attorneys of that city. Recently married, he decided to seek his fortune in the new territory of Oklahoma in April, 1889. With two friends, he "hopped" a freight train two days before the opening. After paying a brakeman to give a slow signal, the trio jumped from the moving train about a mile south of the Guthrie station. Greer told the story of that venture in these words:

"After bidding my wife goodbye and giving her ten of the 39 dollars in my pocket, I went to the home of my mother. Before bidding me goodbye, she said she desired to commit me to the providence of God, Who, she knew, would protect my footsteps and prosper my future...

"I recollect my thoughts on leaving the house—with that prayer fresh in my mind and tears still in my eyes, of the peculiar ambitions of a young man starting into a new country with but 29 dollars in his pocket and nothing but this amount of cash capital and the hopes and prayers of a sainted mother and a loving wife on which to found a newspaper business, and expecting as firmly to found it as if he had a million with which to do it."

Greer's mother arrived on the first train in Guthrie on April 22, acquired a lot on East Oklahoma, and sold it two days later for $90. Meantime, Frank had set up a printshop in a tent—supplies having arrived meantime by wagon.

"She brought the 90 dollars down to the *State Capital* tent," he continued, "and, handing the money to me, said, 'Frank, the Lord has answered $90 worth of my prayer for you on the night you started for Oklahoma.' And the $90 assisted in founding the *State Capital*."

Althought a "sooner" himself, Greer crusaded editorially against the land claimants who had jumped the gun on the opening day. In the forefront of every campaign to build Guthrie, he developed the *Capital* into the leading paper of the territory. When fire destroyed his plant, with $200,000 loss 12 years later, Greer had only $26,000 in insurance. Guthrie citizens raised $50,000, which he accepted as a loan, and he rebuilt. His building, still standing in Guthrie, significantly is topped by a miniature capitol dome.

From Guthrie, Greer went to Tulsa where he amassed a fortune in the oil royalty business. When reverses overtook the business in the depression, he signed over his $60,000 home and other personal holdings to reimburse the stockholders. Greer outlived Haskell only a month and a day, dying August 8, 1933.

Walter Ferguson paid this parting tribute to the pioneer editor:

"Setting about to make Guthrie the dominant city of Oklahoma territory, Greer faced every form of townsite rivalry and railroad promotion and built the most colorful, glamorous and picturesque that the Pioneer West ever knew—went down the long, long trail to statehood when the political changes that, in those days, meant so much to the existence of a newspaper, brought the end to his effort. His paper died in a hopeless fight, with its back against the wall, trying to save the city which he had almost built with his own hands and which was the child of his brilliant mind. He refused to see that Guthrie, the Republican city, was doomed as the future capital of the future Democratic state of Oklahoma, to which Indian territory had been added, and he went down with his colors flying and his face to the enemy."

Re-elected in 1910, Kate Barnard received a $1,000 salary raise from the Third legislature in the special session for locating the capital. Despite the objections of some members that such action would be unconstitutional—coming after the November 8 election—the salary for the Commissioner of Charities and Corrections was boosted to $2,500 a year.

Miss Barnard served a second term, then retired to private life, but continued her efforts to help the down-trodden and friendless. She was found dead in the bathtub in an Oklahoma City hotel Feb. 23, 1930, leaving behind an unusual will which she had written Feb. 22, 1927.

"I give my soul to God," wrote the devoutly religious Miss Barnard. "I bequeath the example of my public life to the youth of the world, praying they may emulate me in dedicating their own lives to securing justice for the poor of their generation as I did in mine."

It is sad to relate, but the probate judge rejected the will. He held there had been too many alterations and interlineations after the document was executed. So her bequest for a "Barnard Home for the Friendless" was disallowed, and the $23,000 estate went to three half brothers.

APPENDIX I

Delegates to the Constitutional Convention

Democrats Unless Otherwise Designated

Districts 1 to 55

Oklahoma Territory

1. T. O. James, Guymon
2. Fred C. Tracy, Beaver
3. Edward R. Williams, Stockholm
4. Homer P. Covey (R), Fargo
5. E. O. McCance, Mutual
6. Dr. G. N. Bilby, Alva
7. John C. Major, Granton
8. George W. Wood, Cherokee
9. D. G. Harned, Ringwood
10. William F. Hendricks, Wakita
11. Charles H. Pittman, Enid
12. J. A. Alderson, Pond Creek
13. Charles L. Moore, Enid
14. Albert H. Ellis, Orlando
15. D. S. Rose, Blackwell
16. Joseph F. King, Newkirk
17. Henry S. Johnston, Perry
18. George M. Berry, Pawnee
19. Dr. E. G. Newell, Yale
20. J. E. Sater (R), Stillwater
21. E. T. Houston (R), Agra
22. Joel M. Sandlin, Prague
23. Rev. Henry L. Cloud (R), Wellston
24. W. L. Helton, Marshall
25. Henry E. Asp (R), Guthrie
26. William D. Jenkins (R), Guthrie
27. W. T. S. Hunt, Oklahoma City
28. W. C. Hughes, Oklahoma City
29. John L. Mitch, Oklahoma City
30. Silas M. Ramsey, Tecumseh
31. James H. Maxey, Shawnee
32. Isaac B. Littleton, Earlsboro
33. T. Charles Wyatt, Wanette
34. J. S. Buchanan, Norman

Districts 57 to 111

Indian Territory

57. Joseph J. Curl, Bartlesville
58. Walter D. Humphrey, Nowata
59. W. H. Kornegay, Nowata
60. Don P. Wills, Chelsea
61. J. W. Swartz, Chelsea
62. Riley Copeland, Fairland
63. J. K. Hill, Catoosa
64. Clement V. Rogers, Claremore
65. J. Howard Langley, Pryor Creek
66. J. Turner Edmondson, Maysville, Ark.
67. Rev. J. H. N. Cobb (R), Sapulpa
68. Flowers Nelson, Tulsa
69. William T. Dalton, Broken Arrow
70. A. L. Hausen, Coweta
71. James A. Harris (R), Wagoner
72. Albert S. Wyly, Tahlequah
73. Charles W. Board, Okfuskee
74. W. A. Cain (R), Oktaha
75. Philip B. Hopkins (R), Muskogee
76. Charles N. Haskell, Muskogee
77. O. P. Brewer, Webber Falls
78. W. N. Littlejohn, Sallisaw
79. William B. Hudson (R), Henryetta
80. H. G. Turner, Brush Hill
81. J. A. Baker, Wewoka
82. E. F. Messenger, Holdenville
83. William C. Liedtke, Eufaula
84. C. O. Frye, Sallisaw
85. Samuel W. Hayes, Chickasha
86. Charles M. McClain, Purcell
87. Carlton Weaver, Ada

35. Jacob K. Norton, Piedmont
36. John J. Carney, El Reno
37. Matthew J. Kane, Kingfisher
38. Thad. D. Rice, Hitchcock
39. Charles C. Fisher, Hinton
40. Henry Kelley, Minco
41. C. H. Bowers, Cement
42. Hymon O. Tener, Taloga
43. David Hogg, Grand
44. W. S. Dearing, Thomas
45. John B. Harrison, Sayre
46. F. E. Herring, Elk City
47. B. E. Bryant, Gotebo
48. J. J. Savage, McKnight
49. Luke Roberts, Olustee
50. W. J. Caudill, Hobart
51. W. E. Banks, Hess
52. James B. Tosh, Hobart
53. William H. Edley, Fletcher
54. John M. Carr, Frederick
55. G. M. Tucker, Comanche
56. T. J. Leahy, Pawhuska, and J. J. Quarles, Fairfax (Osage Nation)
88. Ben F. Harrison, Calvin
89. James S. Wood, Scipio
90. Pete Hanraty, McAlester
91. Neil B. Gardner, Stigler
92. E. T. Sorrels, Milton
93. Royal J. Allen, Duncan
94. Miles Lasater, Pauls Valley
95. Frank J. Stone (I), Wynnewood
96. C. S. Leeper, Sulphur
97. Boone Williams, Lehigh
98. Albert G. Cochran, Hartshorne
99. James S. Latimer, Wilburton
100. C. C. Mathis, Monroe
101. Cham Jones, Ryan
102. J. L. Akers, Woodford
103. Walter A. Ledbetter, Ardmore
104. William H. Murray, Tishomingo
105. James H. Chambers, Atoka
106. J. C. Graham, Marietta
107. George A. Henshaw, Madill
108. R. L. Williams, Durant
109. Gabe E. Parker, Academy
110. B. F. Lee, Hugo
111. Freeman J. McClure (R), Lutfata

APPENDIX II

How the Counties Were Named

When the Organic Act was passed in 1890 establishing a government for Oklahoma territory, seven counties were outlined and designated by number. As other counties were added, with subsequent land openings, the new counties were designated by letters of the alphabet. Later, by vote of the people, county names were adopted. In one instance, the letter "K" was just changed to Kay, while "D" became Dewey.

In the *Chronicles of Oklahoma* for March, 1924, J. B. Thoburn, pioneer historian, traced the origin of the 77 county names.

The first seven counties, designated by number, later took the following names: Logan, Cleveland, Oklahoma, Canadian, Kingfisher, Payne and Beaver.

When the Kiowa-Comanche and Wichita-Caddo reservations were opened to settlement in 1901, the Secretary of the Interior caused the boundaries of the three counties to be defined and their names assigned by executive proclamation. They are Caddo, Comanche and Kiowa.

The Constitutional Convention named the counties formed from old Indian territory, together with several new counties formed from portions of Oklahoma territory. The 75 counties at statehood have been increased to 77 by formation of Harmon and Cotton counties, while Swanson county, organized in 1909, and recognized by Governor Haskell's proclamation of Aug. 13, 1910, was dissolved under an adverse supreme court decision in 1911.

And here's the origin of the county names as traced by Mr. Thoburn:

Adair—for a prominent Cherokee family of which perhaps the most noted member was Col. William Penn Adair.

Alfalfa—for "Alfalfa Bill" Murray.

Atoka—for noted Choctaw sub-chief.

Beaver—named for its principal stream which, in turn, was the English translation of Spanish word "nutria," the name given to the stream because of many beaver dams on its tributaries.

Beckham—for J. C. W. Beckham, former governor of Kentucky.

Blaine—for James G. Blaine, former U. S. senator and once near-winner as presidential nominee.

Bryan—for William Jennings Bryan.

Caddo—for Indian tribe of same name.

Carter—for Capt. Ben W. Carter, a Cherokee Indian who married and settled among the Chickasaws.

Cherokee—for Indian tribe of same name.

Choctaw—for Indian tribe.

Cimarron—for the river; the name is based on a Spanish word meaning wild or unruly.

Cleveland—for President Grover Cleveland.

Coal—for large coal deposits.

Comanche—for Indian tribe.

Cotton—for one of county's staple crops.

Craig—for Granville Craig, prominent citizen of Welch, Okla.

Creek—for Indian tribe.

Custer—for Gen. George A. Custer.

Delaware—for Delaware district of old Cherokee nation.

Dewey—in 1898 voters changed "D" to Dewey in honor of Admiral George Dewey.

Ellis—for Albert H. Ellis, second vice president of Constitutional Convention.

Garfield—for President James A. Garfield.

Garvin—for Samuel Garvin of Pauls Valley, prominent intermarried citizen of Chickasaw nation.

Grady—for Henry W. Grady of Atlanta, Ga., distinguished editor and orator.

Grant—for President U. S. Grant.

Greer—for Lt. Gov. John A. Greer of Texas, by Texas legislature in 1860. It was claimed as part of Texas until supreme court decision in 1895, after which vast area was annexed to Oklahoma territory.

Harmon—for Judson Harmon, former U. S. attorney general and later governor of Ohio; when Greer was annexed by Oklahoma, it was at Harmon's suggestion settlers were permitted to buy additional quarter section adjoining their homesteads at nominal price.

Harper—for O. G. Harper, a clerk in the Constitutional Convention.

Haskell—for C. N. Haskell.

Hughes—for William C. Hughes, Oklahoma City, delegate to the Constitutional Convention.

Jackson—for President Andrew Jackson.

Jefferson—for President Thomas Jefferson.

Johnston—for Douglas H. Johnston, governor of the Chickasaws.

Kay—thrifty voters changed "K" to Kay, saved on printing new county records.

Kingfisher—for King Fisher, early day cattleman, or for the piscatorial bird; local authorities favor cattle man.

Kiowa—for Indian tribe.

Latimer—for J. S. Latimer, delegate to convention.

LeFlore—for Choctaw Indian family of French descent.

Lincoln—for President Abraham Lincoln.

Logan—for Gen. John A. Logan.

Love—for Overton "Sobe" Love of prominent Chickasaw family.

McClain—for Charles McClain, delegate to convention.

McCurtain—for prominent Choctaw family.

McIntosh—for prominent Creek Indian family.

Major—for John C. Major, delegate to the convention.

Marshall—for mother of George A. Henshaw, delegate to convention.

Mayes—for prominent Cherokee family.

Murray—for William H. Murray, only man for whom two counties were named.

Muskogee—for Muscogee or Creek tribe of Indians.

Noble—for John W. Noble, Secretary of Interior in President Harrison's cabinet.

Okfuskee—for Creek Indian clan.

Oklahoma—combination of two Choctaw words, "Okla," meaning people, and "humma," red.

Okmulgee—for Creek Indian clan.

Osage—for Indian tribe.

Ottawa—a tribal name, corruption of "Adawe," meaning to trade or traffic.

Pawnee—a tribal name corrupted from "Pariki," meaning horn; word refers to custom of dressing the scalp locks to resemble a buffalo horn.

Payne—for Capt. David L. Payne, leader of the "boomers".

Pittsburg—for Pittsburgh, Pa., with "h" dropped.

Pontotoc—for Pontotoc creek in old Chickasaw country in Mississippi.

Pottawatomie—for Indian tribe.

Pushmataha—for great Choctaw chieftain.

Roger Mills—for Roger Q. Mills, U. S. senator from Texas.

Rogers—for Clement V. Rogers, member of the convention and father of Will Rogers.

Seminole—for Indian tribe.

Sequoyah—for Indian who invented Cherokee alphabet.

Stephens—for John H. Stephens, Texas congressman.

Texas—so named because panhandle strip belonged to Texas until 1850.

Tillman—for Ben Tillman, U. S. senator from South Carolina.

Tulsa—for Tulsey Town, one of old Creek towns or clans.

Wagoner—named for county seat, which in turn was named for Bailey P. Wagoner, railroad attorney.

Washington—for President George Washington.

Washita—for Washita river; apparently corrupt spelling of French "Faux Ouachita," as distinguished from true Ouachita in Arkansas.

Woods—for Samuel N. Wood, Kansas legislator killed two years before Cherokee strip opening; "s" inadvertently added on ballot.

Woodward—for B. W. Woodward, Santa Fe railroad director, for whom city of Woodward was named.

Index